ACHIEVING
BY THE YE.

CW00375432

As the world nears the end of this millennium wracked with conflict and violence, the abolition of war by the year 2000 must seem a daunting task – but, argues the author, it is a realistic timetable for the conclusion of a series of interlinked treaties, the first vital steps towards world peace. In the face of seemingly insurmountable global problems, with the threat of a nuclear holocaust looming ever larger on the horizon, many people have become cynical, fatalistic and discouraged. Yet in this highly topical book, John Huddleston puts forward a coherent vision of a more hopeful future and a convincing assessment of what must be done to achieve it.

John Huddleston is Chief of the Budget and Planning Division of the International Monetary Fund (IMF), where he has worked since 1963. Born in Manchester, England, before the Second World War, he spent five years working for the British Ministry of Defence before moving to Washington. He is the author of *The Earth is but One Country*.

ACHIEVING PEACE BY THE YEAR 2000

A Twelve Point Proposal

John Huddleston

Chief of the Budget and Planning Division
of the International Monetary Fund

O N E W O R L D

ACHIEVING PEACE BY THE YEAR 2000

Oneworld Publications Ltd
1c Standbrook House, Old Bond St, London W1X 3TD

British Library Cataloguing in Publication Data
Huddleston, John
Achieving Peace by the Year 2000: a twelve point proposal
1. Peace
I. Title
327.1'72   JX1952

ISBN 1–85168–006–3

Printed and bound in Great Britain

'What can be done to establish goals that are appropriate to the present global situations of mankind? Every individual citizen of planet Earth should face this question, for each person can play a meaningful and important role in promoting the healthy transformations of values and goals.'

From *A Report to the Club of Rome*, 1977[1]

Contents

Preface   ix

PART ONE   ATTITUDES TO PEACE
1   Peace and the Superpowers   3
2   The Causes of War and the Paths to Peace   10

PART TWO   A BLUEPRINT FOR PEACE
3   Twelve Proposals for World Peace   49
        (1)   A world peace constituency   50
        (2)   A world peace assembly   53
        (3)   The outlawing of war   54
        (4)   The abolition of offensive weapons   56
        (5)   Sanctions against aggressors   65
        (6)   A World Peace Council   69
        (7)   Compulsory arbitration of disputes   72
        (8)   An international peace force   76
        (9)   An independent peace fund   78
       (10)   An equal role for women in the
              peace process   80
       (11)   Education of world citizens   82
       (12)   Reduction of international tensions   82

PART THREE   PRACTICAL CONSIDERATIONS
4   A Timetable for Peace   87
5   The Global Challenge and the Individual   90
6   Summary   92

APPENDICES
  I : The Quest for Peace: A Short History   97
 II : Statistics on War and Peace   121
III : Peace Questionnaire   127

Notes   130
Bibliography   138

Preface

This short book has two main purposes. The first is to try and make a useful contribution to the discussion of the practical aspects of achieving world peace. The method is to discuss links between on the one hand 'soft' approaches to peace such as the promotion of general values relating to the idea of the oneness of humanity and on the other 'hard' approaches such as international treaties and other diplomatic initiatives. Experience over the last hundred years strongly suggests that both approaches are necessary and that the work of establishing peace will not be effective until the two are closely linked. By itself the 'soft' approach produces little practical action in the short run; conversely, when the 'hard' approach is pursued in isolation from the 'soft', although tangible results may be produced, these are usually hollow and easily shatter.

The second purpose is to move beyond discussion into action. This means encouraging every reader to consider how he or she can actively work for peace. Peace affects us all and is too important a part of our lives to be left to politicians and soldiers. The more people there are actively working for peace worldwide, the more likely will be the possibility of its realization. Some of us may have greater opportunities to serve the peace process than others – but everyone, no matter how humble in self-assessment, can make a valuable contribution. It is such a point of view that has prompted this essay by someone who is neither directly involved in diplomacy nor a political scientist.

It should be stressed that the specific proposals made here are not intended as the perfect solution but merely as a starting point for discussion. Readers are encouraged to examine the suggestions critically and to search out any flaws. However, the book would be a failure if the reader stopped there. The challenge to the reader is to devise better suggestions for achieving peace if the proposals seem unrealistic or otherwise flawed.

The writer takes full responsibility for all that is contained in these pages, but it must be acknowledged that the suggestions made here have been largely inspired by the principles of the Bahá'í Faith. This should not be a surprise to the reader, for surely few would deny that the original teachings of all the great religions have always been a potent force for peace in the world. That universal theme is a prominent facet of the Bahá'í Faith, the most recent of the world religions – a point briefly discussed in Appendix I, which summarizes some of the highlights of the peace movement during the last two centuries. The Bahá'í view of peace has been given wide publicity in a statement entitled *The Promise of World Peace*[2] which was issued in 1985 by the Universal House of Justice, the supreme council of the Bahá'í world community, in connection with the United Nations International Year of Peace. In a sense this essay is a small personal footnote to that profound document. Having said all this, it should be added that, although occasional references to the Bahá'í Faith occur, this book is intended for a universal audience, regardless of beliefs – indeed, for all those who are concerned with bringing about an end to war and the establishment of lasting peace.

PART ONE

Attitudes to Peace

CHAPTER 1

Peace and the Superpowers

Over the last hundred years efforts to end war between nations and to establish peace on earth have been gathering momentum. The movement has included vast numbers of private citizens as well as diplomats and statesmen, and their views have been eloquently expressed in conferences and conventions, academic studies, diplomatic initiatives, appeals in the news media, demonstrations, 'sit-ins' and marches throughout the world. The discussion has ranged across such subjects as international consultation, international law, the mediation and arbitration of international disputes, the outlawing of war, collective security, an international police force, multilateral and unilateral disarmament, the removal of extremes of wealth and poverty between nations and the elimination of abuses of human rights and dignity. The highlights of the movement have included the establishment of first the League of Nations and later the United Nations, the creation of a World Court, cooperation between nations for mutual benefit on a vast range of technical matters, a Universal Declaration of Human Rights, and the organization of economic assistance to materially less well-off countries through multilateral agencies. There can be no question

3

that, taken as a whole, the movement has made the world a better place than it would otherwise have been. The vast and growing network of international contacts and cooperation at both government and private levels have undoubtedly improved the long-term prospects of peace. For millions, war with their neighbours is now inconceivable. (A brief account of the peace movement and the evolution of international cooperation is given in Appendix I.)

And yet everywhere there is disappointment. Despite the fact that two world wars have been fought 'to end war', the world is still wracked by international conflict. It is estimated that in the forty years since World War II some 15 million people have lost their lives in over a hundred wars and armed conflicts. At the time of writing a major war rages in the Middle East, extreme tensions threaten the eruption of international war in half a dozen other locations, and a multitude of civil wars simmer continuously, erupting periodically into large-scale conflicts.[3] Worst of all, hanging over humanity like the sword of Damocles is the threat of a nuclear holocaust, a disaster on an unimaginable scale. Five nations between them possess more than 50,000 nuclear weapons, and half a dozen other nations may soon have such weapons if they do not secretly possess them already. There is an immense risk from cold-blooded calculation on the part of men who have lost all sense of proportion, from misunderstanding , from miscalculation or from sheer accident. It is hardly surprising that the rising generation is fearful of the future.

However, in the last two to three years there have been at least two developments that offer the hope of something better than the destruction of civilization. The first has been the United Nations International

Year of Peace (1985–6), which showed that yearning for peace and support for a peace movement was more widespread than ever before. The deep feelings roused by the peace movement are described by Jonathan Schell in his book *The Abolition:* 'This awakening is new, and its extent and its consequences are still uncertain, but it promises to be one of those great changes of heart in mankind – such as the awakening to the evil of slavery in the nineteenth century.'[4]

Suspicion that 'peace talk' was just a propaganda drive against Western interests is no longer much in evidence. Even in the Communist countries ordinary people are beginning to voice not only concern but criticism of government for putting the world at risk with their policies, and their concern has been echoed by the Soviet leader, Mikhail Gorbachev:

> I feel we should really ponder whether we might not be lagging behind the sentiments, the feelings of our peoples, because these sentiments are centainly in favour of the two countries [the USA and the USSR] and peoples drawing closer together. . . . You know I am really thrilled by the fact that our kids . . . how profoundly, how deeply aware they are that something needs to be done and they certainly have many complaints which they address to us.[5]

No doubt an important factor in these developments has been the publication in the early 1980s of scientific theories about a nuclear winter which seek to demonstrate that the explosion of only a few hundred of the thousands of weapons available would create such a dense dust cloud in the upper atmosphere that it would blot out the sun for many months, thus causing a drastic fall in average temperatures and widespread crop failure throughout the northern hemisphere and possibly the southern hemisphere as well. In short, it was clearer than ever before that there could be no winners in a nuclear war; an attacker would destroy his own country as well as that of the enemy, even if the enemy never retaliated. The record, over forty years, of governments consistently underestimating (at least in public) the devastating effect of nuclear explosions gives credence to this theory, and the point was given additional emphasis by the disaster at the Chernobyl nuclear power plant which showed in a very immediate way that the dangers are not just scientfic theory but a day-to-day reality.

The second development which gives hope that humanity can still avoid a nuclear holocaust has been the recent round of disarmament negotiations between the two superpowers: the Intermediate Nuclear Forces Treaty (INF) and the proposed Strategic Arms Reduction Treaty (START). There have been arms treaties between the superpowers before, notably the two Strategic Arms Limitation Treaties (SALT I and II), the Anti-Ballistic Missile Treaty (ABM) and the Partial Test Ban Treaty (see Appendix I). What is distinctive about the present round of negotiations is that for the first time they involve an actual reduction in the existing number of weapons and not just a ceiling on future growth in numbers. They also provide for much improved means of verifying that both sides are abiding by the terms of the treaty. This is an extremely important feature, because in such critical matters neither side could risk merely relying on the word of the other. Hitherto, the Soviet Union has always opposed comprehensive verification procedures in its territories. It may well be that one reason for the recent change to a more accommodating position reflects the confidence that comes from the attainment of approximate parity in nuclear weapons with the United States in the last few years.

There are several reasons for believing that the present advance in disarmament negotiations may not be a passing phase but rather the beginning of what may be a long-term trend towards reduced tension between the superpowers. One factor is that scientific evidence and nuclear parity have combined to make it clear that for rational persons nuclear weapons are quite useless, and their only conceivable value is to deter use of such weapons by another nation. It is not only nuclear weapons that are becoming less useful: there is growing doubt about the value of the total military strength of the superpowers. Experiences in Vietnam and Afghanistan have shown both superpowers how limited can be the usefulness of their conventional military forces. At the same time, there is growing consciousness of the heavy financial burden of military power which escalates with each succeeding generation of weapons. It is estimated that the Soviet Union spends about 15 per cent of her GNP on defence and the USA about 7 per cent, as compared with an average for the Western European industrial countries of 3 to 5 per cent and for Japan, the third largest national economy in the world, less than 1 per cent. (See Appendix II for some basic statistics on war and peace today.) Such a large expense, year in and year out, is perceived as a major drag on the economies of the superpowers which reduces their economic strength vis-à-vis other nations, quite apart from the substantive issues involved. This is at a time when it is increasingly evident that a powerful economy rather than a powerful military is the real practical day-to-day source of influ-

7

ence in international affairs.[6] In short, both super-powers are beginning to find that massive armaments may be a source of weakness rather than of strength.

Of course, the positive developments in popular yearning for peace and in armaments negotiations have to be viewed with a degree of caution. It would be foolhardy to think that suddenly everything is going to be well with the world. The peace movement is still ephemeral: there is no hard-core majority constituency in either the USA or the Soviet Union, let alone in other countries, nor are peace organizations united and some still pursue narrow political agendas which ignore the wider picture. As for détente between the superpowers, there remains much suspicion and a compulsion to confront one another and to exploit one another's diffi-culties at every possible opportunity – a tendency which is strongly reinforced by ideological antagonisms. (However, as an aside, the writer would hazard the suggestion that, after raging for seventy years or so, the ideological battles are now beginning to lose some of their fire as they become increasingly irrelevant to the present-day situation.) The treaties themselves will still leave thousands of nuclear weapons in the hands of the superpowers – the INF will eliminate about 3 to 4 per cent of the total number and START some 50 per cent of strategic as distinct from tactical weapons – not to speak of the weapons which other nuclear nations will continue to possess. In other words, nuclear war will still be a possibility.

How then to come to a conclusion? The most constructive approach would surely be to view the growing support for peace coupled with progress in disarmament negotiations as an opportunity to be grasped while it is still there, and to start pressing for further steps along the path to a lasting and comprehensive world peace. The dangers in the present situation should be given full recognition – not in order to freeze into cynical inaction, but rather to ensure that our thinking about the future is practical and down-to-earth as well as visionary. In the final analysis, humanity has a choice: establish peace on the basis of rational consultation – or have peace enforced by disaster. If the first option is our choice, then it is clear that peace has to be the highest priority as a matter of principle and all other concerns must take second place.

CHAPTER 2

The Causes of War and the Paths to Peace

There would appear to be at least two general aspects of war and peace that should be reviewed as a background to any specific proposals for promoting the advancement of the peace process.

The first general aspect is the ultimate long-term objective. It is not enough to make ad hoc policies, reacting to every twist and turn as we go along. As former US Secretary of State, Dr Henry Kissinger, commented recently:

> The arms race is a symptom of tensions that go back at least 40 years and transcend personalities. I do not believe that peace is as easy to establish as a mood. A change of conduct is needed, an end to the tendency to exploit every dissatisfaction to weaken the existing structures. The United States and the Soviet Union should see what kind of a world we want in the year 2000, and if we agree, work back from there.[7]

It goes without saying that the achievement of a lasting

peace is far too complex a task to be achieved in one mighty stroke. Inevitably, it is a process involving a multitude of steps. Long-term objectives and goals are necessary to give a sense of purpose and direction, and to ensure that each step along the path of peace is consistent with the others. Without such goals it is all too easy to become diverted down meandering byways and distracted by the shallow gimmicks of political hoopla. Treaties for disarmament and international cooperation, for example, are not to be seen as grudging concessions, with argument over sentence, clause and comma, but rather as part of a long-term process which is constructive and for the advantage of all. Some very general long-term perspectives are therefore touched upon at the end of this chapter.

The second general aspect of war and peace that needs to be discussed is an analysis of the main causes of war and what general conclusions there might be regarding their solution. This is obviously a complex subject which can be discussed from many points of view and at many levels, ranging from basic human emotions such as fear, anger, ambition, greed and hatred to major historical forces, such as population changes and migrations, and such philosophical concepts as the legitimacy of waging a war in order to achieve or defend freedom or economic and social justice. The approach taken here will be to eschew philosophical theory and to concentrate on more practical matters relevant to the immediate problem of making the world safe for humanity. These matters are the political, social and economic factors that can be seen as common themes running through the international conflicts of modern times: nationalism, racism, extremes of wealth and poverty, religious fanaticism and strife, male domination of public affairs, and

11

competitive arms races. The solutions discussed are at the level of basic attitudes to public affairs: views about human nature, national sovereignty and the unity of mankind. Such views are crucial in tackling the problem of how best to build world peace.

Nationalism

Few would argue against the proposition that nationalism is one of the most powerful forces which cause war in the modern world. It was certainly one of the most important factors leading up to both world wars. Nationalism has proved itself powerful enough to split the Communist block, although supposedly united against the capitalist nations, and it is a major ingredient in nearly all the wars, both hot and cold, raging in the world today.

Nationalism might be described as a decadent form of patriotism. Patriotism itself is historically and emotionally closely linked to the idea of democracy, and represents the legitimate desire of a people to express their own culture free from outside influence or domination. When such feelings are focused on self-respect and give confidence enough for other cultures to be viewed in a friendly way, they are clearly beneficial for the spiritual and material development of humanity. However, patriotism, a noble sense of social solidarity, deteriorates into mere nationalism when it becomes intertwined with ignorance, fear and hatred of other peoples.

There are several degrees to the decadence of patriotism. Many have argued that when the people of a country rise in armed rebellion to achieve independence they are waging a 'just war'. Sometimes the patriots are the vast majority in a country rebelling against an alien occupier – for example, in nineteenth-century Latin America and Italy or twentieth-century Algeria and Vietnam. Sometimes the national group is a minority fighting to carve out a territorial corner for itself – e.g. the Kurds, the Tamils and the Basques. Whatever the situation, a so-called just war is still a war in which thousands of men, women and children innocent of personal responsibility for oppression are sacrificed by those drunk with their own patriotism. The reality behind the romantic story in the history book is not always pretty.

But decadent patriotism can sink to a much lower level when it seeks to assert itself by active aggression against another people. Often this will mean suppression of minority groups within the national territory, such as the Hungarian oppression of Slav minorities in the nineteenth century or the persecution of the Turkish minority in Bulgaria today. At other times it will lead a nation to seize neighbouring territory, using such excuses as historical right, the need for space for an expanding population or simple fear that this is the only way to prevent an attack by others. The division of Poland by Prussia, Russia and Austria in the late eighteenth century is one example; the occupation of most of Europe by Germany in the 1940s is another. Indeed, Hitler justified Germany's invasion of her neighbours in the following terms: 'It is a question of expanding our living space in the east, of securing our food supplies . . . Eighty million people must get what is their right. Their existence must be secured. Might is right.'[8]

The threat of nationalism to the cause of peace goes beyond these obvious situations, however, because nationalism reinforces the idea of the sovereign state. This acts as a heavy brake on efforts to achieve world cooperation for the benefit of all humanity. Immediate apparent gains for the nation, even when quite frivolous, are given priority over long-term benefits for the world, especially if the price is perceived to be a limit on national sovereignty. The superpowers pursue this policy of short-sighted self-interest to even greater extremes: for not only do they jockey for power and influence as an end in itself, regardless of substantive issues, but apparently feel compelled to oppose each other in every region of the globe just because the other nation is a superpower, rather than because there is a direct and vital interest at stake. The genesis and escalation of such power struggles are depicted by H. B. Danesh in *Unity: the Creative Foundation of Peace*:

> Striving for power is often related to fear, with the accompanying need to conceal one's fears from others and, most important, from oneself. However, because power in itself creates more fear, the process evolves into a cycle where one seeks power to feel more secure but, instead, becomes more insecure as a result of the suspicion and envy of others. Eventually, the frustrated and fearful individuals engaged in this process resort to violence in the hope of eliminating the other party or parties involved in the power struggle.[9]

Racism

The murder of six million Jews in the holocaust of World War II and the violence provoked by apartheid in contemporary South Africa are but the most well known examples of racism – a second major cause of war in the modern world. In many respects racism

14

represents a deepening of the fears and hatreds associated with nationalism. Whereas extreme nationalism is essentially about cultural differences such as language, racism implies contempt for other people because of innate physical differences such as the colour of their skin or their facial features. For those on the receiving end of such contempt, particularly children, the result can be devastating, both mentally and spiritually: as noted in *The Promise of World Peace*, 'Racism retards the unfoldment of the boundless potentialities of its victims, corrupts its perpetrators, and blights human progress.'[10]

To some degree the spirit of racism has been present in civilization since the very beginning, but it is only in the last two or three hundred years that it has become a major and all-pervasive affliction of humanity. This development has been largely associated with the rise to dominance of Europe, militarily, politically and economically, as a result of technological innovation. These advantages gave the Europeans such power that by the end of the nineteenth century they had colonized virtually the whole world. Perhaps inevitably, the Europeans came to see themselves as superior to others. This attitude contrasted sharply with their earlier respect for the civilizations of Asia – as evidenced by the changing attitude of the British in India, for example, from the eighteenth to the nineteenth century. This growing feeling of superiority was reinforced by religious institutions which spread the view that non-European religions were false and immoral, and by an interpretation of Darwinian theories about the evolution of man which suggested that the white man was at the highest level of natural evolution. The 'white man's burden', his self-appointed task of ruling the world, came from his perceived moral superiority as well as from his management skills. Later

15

came the more extreme vision of the Aryan 'master race' which had the 'right' to take from 'inferior' species as if by virtue of a law of nature. Such attitudes have not been confined to Nazism, as the experience of American Indians and Australian Aborigines amply demonstrates. Fear added fuel to the fire: the sense of being a minority roused a deep fear in the 'superior' European race that some day they would be overwhelmed by the 'barbarians', as had happened in Ancient Rome. Such fears were usually hidden, but were given overt expression by Kaiser Wilhelm II of Germany when he warned his fellow European monarchs of the hordes from China – the 'Yellow Peril' – though, in reality, it was the Chinese who had reason to fear the Europeans.

Gradually, the full tide of racism began to recede in response to a series of events: the campaign against slavery; the rise of democracy and public education; the horror of the holocaust; the initial defeat of the Western powers by Asians during World War II; the end of the great colonial empires; and the worldwide spread of the civil rights movement. Nevertheless, racism is still a major cause of pain and anguish and a real danger to world peace, for memories of the past linger on both amongst former oppressors and their victims. Like extreme nationalism, it often flourishes most strongly in places where people of different races feel threatened by one another – because, for instance, the poorer group greatly outnumbers the richer, or because they are competing for a limited number of jobs.

Extremes of Wealth and Poverty

It has been obvious from the daily news over the last half century that extremes of wealth and poverty are among the prime causes of war in the modern world.

Attention is drawn to this fact by the gigantic ideological and political struggle between Communism and democratic capitalism. As noted earlier, there are other factors, such as nationalism and the sheer dynamic of power politics, which contribute to the tension between East and West; but these are reinforced by passionate ideological differences about how to solve the problem of poverty and the relative priority of this goal as compared with others, such as the preservation of the democratic process and the liberty of the individual. Since 1917 nearly every continent has been torn by wars caused by differences of view on this issue. In recent decades another dimension has been added to the danger by the confrontation between the industrial countries of the West and Third World nations who argue bitterly that the former have a moral obligation to give them massive economic assitance because their poverty is essentially the result of past colonialism and present neo-colonialism.

Quarrels about ownership and use of wealth have always been one of the most frequent causes of war. One major category of such quarrels has been that between the rich and powerful oppressor on the one hand and the poor and weak on the other – in the majority of instances involving the former plundering the latter – in contrast to the occasional act of retaliation from the poor when driven to extremes of desperation. General passiveness on the part of the poor came from acceptance that it was more or less a law of life that the majority could never expect more than a hand to mouth existence, with the possibility of starvation always there whenever there was a crop failure or some other natural or man-made disaster. This all changed with the coming of the industrial revolution, which gave a promise for the first time in history that with fair and competent

17

management society could ensure a reasonable standard of living for all humanity. As consciousness of this change became widespread, the poor became less willing to passively accept their lot: the very existence of extremes of wealth and poverty was seen as an act of violence in itself. Trade unions, cooperatives and Socialist parties were established to work for a more just economic order. In a minority of democratic societies such organizations were able to make significant changes for the better in a peaceful way. More often, demands for economic justice were resisted and the result was an intensification of social conflict: rebellions, strikes, revolutions, counter-revolutions and oppression.

In the words of *The Promise of World Peace*, 'The inordinate disparity between rich and poor, a source of acute suffering, keeps the world in a state of instability, virtually on the brink of war.'[11]

The impact of the industrial revolution was compounded by two other developments. First, although the European colonization of most of the world during the eighteenth and nineteenth centuries undoubtedly contributed to the welfare of some of the occupied countries (for example, by building roads, railways, dams, hospitals, etc., and the introduction of modern methods of administration), the general impact was that of exploitation, with the European countries using their colonies as markets for their industrial goods and as sources of cheap food and raw materials. Though the colonial era is now over, many of its economic consequences remain; as a result tension and bitterness exist between the two main groups of nations involved. This situation remains a potential source of war – particularly terrorism, that form of warfare which the weak are often obliged to use.

The other development which compounds the tensions that arise from extremes of wealth and poverty has been the massive growth of communications. Newspapers, television and transistor radios in every village daily draw to the attention of the poor the shiny consumer goods which the rich have and they do not. Jet planes from rich countries daily arrive in poor countries and disgorge rich Westerners, bringing with them all the appendages of prosperity. This is not just a question of envy, but of basic fairness and justice: 'Why should I and my people be the ones who are deprived?'

Religious Strife

After briefly considering the more obvious causes of war in the modern world – nationalism, racism, and extremes of wealth and poverty – let us now turn to two factors that are perhaps normally taken less seriously than they deserve but which are in fact of considerable importance: religious strife and the domination of public affairs by men. Two decades of civil war between Catholics and Protestants in Northern Ireland; an ongoing civil war in Lebanon, the factions of which divide along religious lines; the assault on the Golden Temple of Amritsar, the assassination of the Prime Minister of India, Mrs Gandhi, full-scale terrorism in the Punjab, with periodic explosions elsewhere (all in connection with the Sikh–Hindu conflict); and, above all, the resurgence of a fundamentalist and militarist form of Islam in Iran and in other countries in Asia and Africa have all drawn attention to the fact that religion can be a dangerous force in the world. Western society, for the most part now secular, had until recently tended to think that religious strife was no longer a major factor in public affairs. This view reflected a general disenchantment with religion and religious arguments which originated with the bitter wars of the Reformation in Europe during the sixteenth and seventeenth centuries. Some still tend to think that modern religious conflicts are really about 'tribal' affairs rather than religion as such (e.g., in Northern Ireland), but this view is hard to maintain in the face of Islamic fundamentalism. Most informed commentators agree that this is not just a response to Western imperialism but a genuine reaction against the crudities of materialism and the consumer society. There are similar fundamentalist rumblings in other religious communities too, including a revival of fundamentalism among Christians in America. Much of the thrust of such fundamentalist groups is hatred of others and a willingness to use force to achieve their goals. Religion has always been one of the most powerful forces in society; it would be a grave mistake not to take it seriously as a major potential factor for peace or for war.

There is of course a terrible tragic irony in a situation where religion has to be considered a cause of war given the fact that all the founders of the great religions taught that humanity is one spiritual family and we should live together in amity and peace in a law-abiding society. The pattern of history has been that, as established religious institutions have aged, such profound themes have been overcast with concerns about power and a desire by religious leaders that their religion alone be seen as the truth and all others as false. First, in the name of unity, anyone in a religious community who shows independence is persecuted as a heretic – for example, the Cathars in twelfth-century France or the Hussites in sixteenth-century Bohemia. A second manifestation of division is quarrels within a religion between rival sects, such as those between the

Lutherans and Roman Catholics during the European Reformation or between the Shiis and Sunnis during the early centuries of Islam. Finally, there are wars between religions: the Christian crusades against Islam, the forced conversion of Jews by Christians in medieval Spain, the centuries of war between Islam and Hinduism on the Indian subcontinent, etc.

Religion so corrupted and divided has a tendency to narrow-mindedness not only with regard to other religious groups but also with regard to science; superstition becomes rampant, and those in authority anxious to hang on to the trappings of power ally with oppressive governments against the poor. Such institutions and leaders have completely lost the original spirit of their religion and will no doubt eventually be abandoned by the people. Meanwhile, during the process of decadence, they are a serious menace to the peace of the world. The challenge now facing the religious leaders of mankind is to seriously consider, with honesty and compassion, the plight of humanity, and to ask themselves whether they cannot try to submerge their theological differences and work together for the advancement of human understanding and peace.[12]

The Domination of Public Affairs by Men and the Subjection of Women

Growing numbers of men and women believe that another important factor that contributes to the culture of war is the dominance of men in public affairs and the subjection of women. This is a condition that has existed in all societies to a greater or lesser degree since the beginning of civilization.[13] It is true, of course, that in the last hundred years women have won significant advances in public affairs. Most notably, they now have equal voting rights in just about every country in the world where executive and legislative branches of government are elected by the people. Women have also won high office: they have been elected to legislative assemblies, and have become ministers and even in several instances prime ministers during the last two decades. However, it should be noted that the number of women reaching high office has been very small compared with the number of men. Furthermore, there is a general tendency to shunt women off into posts which are not central to the immediate issues of peace. It is, for instance, hard to name many women who have been foreign ministers or ministers of defence. Even the United Nations itself has been slow to appoint women to high office and it was only in 1987 that the first woman was selected to head a UN agency. The absence of women from diplomacy was noted as an important issue at the National Women's Conference held in Washington D.C. at the end of 1987.

Lack of true political equality is only one aspect of sexual inequality and in many countries is a direct reflection of the general esteem in which women are held by society as a whole. In Western democracies, the political advance of women has been paralleled by improvements in their social, legal and economic status that have allowed women to lead a fuller life. The present situation, however, is still far from satisfactory. There are considerable problems, for instance, in reconciling principles of equity and fairness when men and women clearly have particular needs at key points in their lives, especially during maternity and early motherhood. Old prejudices still linger on as is evident from the fact that large numbers of women in all Western nations suffer violence, even within the family.

In most Third World countries the situation is far worse: young girls have a higher death rate than boys, even though they are biologically stronger; they are handicapped by a much lower rate of literacy; and they are often subjected to early arranged marriage, brutal circumcision practices and prostitution. Economically they are an underclass. A recent United Nations survey reports that 'women, while they represent 50 per cent of the world's adult population and one third of the official labour force, perform nearly two thirds of all working hours, receive only one tenth of the world's income, and own less than one per cent of world prosperity.'[14] The failure to involve women at the grass roots level is one of the major flaws in the post-war programme of international social and economic development, and may be a reason why the results have been so disappointing.

There are at least two issues here which are relevant in the context of the peace discussion. The first is a simple matter of justice: why should 50 per cent of the population of the world have an inferior position purely on account of sex? With such inequality on such a vast scale it is easy to slip into injustice to other groups, and that inevitably means discontent and therefore an unstable social environment in which to try to establish peace. Second, and perhaps more important, is the argument that women, precisely because of their sex, have a special contribution to make to the cause of peace. As mothers they carry the foetus within themselves, undergo the pain of birth and have the closest responsibility for children in the early years from breast feeding onwards; women therefore have a natural and powerful concern for the preservation of life, and from that comes a giving and cooperative approach to the family and to the wider community. Also being phys-

23

ically the weaker sex, they have an interest in restraining physical violence. To this line of reasoning derived from their very physiology can be added the argument that traditionally women have always been builders rather than destroyers – being responsible for the management of the home, preparation of food, health care, pottery and weaving, cultivation of land, etc. – and have rarely been involved in killing either in the hunt or in combat with other communities.[15]

Moreover, it is clear from the record that even under the handicap of oppression women have played a major role in modern attempts to make society more humane, caring and peaceful – such as the movements against slavery and for prison reform, trade unions, charities, Socialism, health care and housing management, and campaigns concerning the environment, temperance and human rights. As the authors of *Women's Choices*, published in 1983, observe: 'Women do tend to notice, and to show grave emotional evils which men prefer to conceal.'[16] Women have taken special initiatives in the peace movement itself such as the Greenham Common demonstrations in England and the forming of the Northern Ireland Peace Movement by Mairead Corrigan and Betty Williams, who were awarded the Nobel Peace Prize in 1976. Margaret Thatcher, the British Prime Minister, coined the epigram 'In politics, if you want anything said, ask a man; if you want anything done, ask a woman.'[17] The record of women as effective activists both for peace and humanitarian causes in general is summed up by the authors of *Women in the World*, published in 1986:

The gender gap at the polls has since become an important factor in elections in the USA. Women's voting records show that they are more likely to

24

favour stronger environmental protection regulation, gun control, abolition of the death penalty, and are more likely to vote against weapons build-ups.[18]

Generally, it is not women that glory in war, dress up in fancy military uniforms, devour war books, commit violent crimes or kill wild animals for the fun of it.

This, of course, is not to say that all women are peaceful: in the harsh struggle to rise in a male-dominated world many women have put aside feminine qualities. Nor are all men aggressive and warlike: many men have worked for peace and other movements to make society more humane and caring. What is being argued is that women as a whole, on the basis of their collective experience and way of life for thousands of years, have demonstrated that they can be an extremely powerful force for peace if encouraged to take their rightful place in public affairs. As *The Promise of World Peace* puts it:

> The denial of such equality perpetrates an injustice against one half of the world's population and promotes in men harmful attitudes and habits that are carried from the family to the workplace, to political life, and ultimately to international relations . . . Only as women are welcomed into full partnership in all fields of human endeavour will the moral and psychological climate be created in which international peace can emerge.[19]

The point is given added force when one considers what has happened in societies that have been extreme in their belittling of women. The notorious suppression of women in Second Empire Germany was the reverse

25

side of a male cult of militarism – a factor which in itself contributed to the mad rush to World War I – and the subjection of women again coincided with militarism under the Nazis. Nor is it purely coincidental that in the present day a regime which spews our hatred for the rest of the world and practises secret midnight tortures and executions on its own citizens also makes a point of striving to reverse the advances achieved by women.

Arms Competitions

The last general cause of war to be discussed here is the phenomenon of arms races and active preparations for war during peacetime. There is a general view that arms races are not in themselves a root cause of war but merely a symptom of mistrust or hostility. Clearly, to a considerable degree that is true: peoples would not arm against each other if there were mutual trust. Nevertheless, experience suggests that armaments races add significantly to international tension and on occasion can be the critical factor that tips the balance between peace and war. The typical progression is described by the diplomat and historian George Kennan:

I see this competitive build-up of armaments conceived initially as a means to an end but soon becoming an end in itself. I see it taking possession of men's imagination and behaviour, becoming a force in its own right, detaching itself from the political differences that initially inspired it, and then leading both parties, invariably and inexorably, to the war they no longer know how to avoid.[20]

26

Thus in 1914, after the assassination at Sarajevo, the great powers were so well armed that they were able to undertake major military campaigns almost immediately, and the main concern was to strike as soon as possible – as in the case of the German Schleiffen Plan to outmanoeuvre the French army – with the hope of catching the other side off guard. The diplomats were given no time to try to work out a peaceful settlement of the crisis. Similarly, in 1939 the Nazi government had every incentive to strike quickly against the Western Powers, who lagged behind Germany in rearmament; and against Russia, whose officer corps had just been decimated by Stalin's 'Great Purge'. In the nuclear age, there is constant fear that one or other of the superpowers will acquire first strike capability – i.e. the ability to knock out all the other side's nuclear weapons in one swoop, thus pre-empting the possibility of retaliatory action. The fear is that if one side did acquire such a capability, it would be tempted to use it so as to eliminate once and for all any further risk of an attack by the other side.

Though this is the most immediate problem, there is also an additional factor in so far as arms races are very expensive (today between 5 and 6 per cent of the world's total annual product is spent on military affairs) and divert resources away from more productive ends such as reducing the incidence of poverty – which, as noted earlier, is one of the most potent causes of war.

The Nature of Man

To eliminate these general causes of war there have to be some fundamental changes in the way we think. The first such change concerns the prevalent view of human nature – which regards man as innately selfish, uncaring and violent. Such a view has a crippling effect on efforts to achieve peace because it suggests that nothing will ever change and that therefore it is a waste of time to try to alter the way governments think or behave: all that can be done is to 'carry a big stick' and hope that this will deter would-be aggressors.

This perspective has become deeply embedded in Western culture as a result of the teachings of the Christian churches that man has been sinful since the expulsion from the Garden of Eden and that he can only be saved through the sacrifice of Jesus. It is a view that has been confirmed and deepened by materialistic philosophy, which ultimately puts emphasis on hedonism and selfishness. Materialistic philosophers have pointed to the aggressiveness of certain animals and from this base argue that man must also be naturally aggressive. The beginnings of a more positive view of human nature was taught by the philosophers of the French Enlightenment, who held that man in nature is essentially good and has only been corrupted by bad government: change government and all would be well with the world. Such optimism finally lost credibility after the horrors of two world wars and the holocaust of European Jewry, with the realization that governments could not have carried out such vast atrocities without the connivance of millions of individual human beings.

And yet as we let our natural reaction to these terrible events settle into perspective, it is clear that a totally negative view of human nature simply does not give a full explanation of the history of civilization. How, for instance, can total pessimism be reconciled with the voluntary abolition of slavery and the establishment of great charities in the nineteenth century; with the widespread support for human rights and concern for the starving of Africa today; or with such inspiring men

28

and women of history as King Ashoka of India, St Francis of Assisi, Florence Nightingale, Eleanor Roosevelt, Raoul Wallenberg, Albert Schweitzer, Mahatma Gandhi, Abraham Lincoln, Dag Hammarskjöld and Mother Teresa? A pessimistic view is also contradicted by evidence amassed by anthropologists showing that 'human nature' or 'basic human values' can vary greatly from one society and environment to another. Modern Western individualism and the war culture of advanced civilization has not been the universal experience. Many tribes of Africa, the Americas and Australasia have put emphasis on the holding of property by the community rather than by individuals, and have ritualized conflict with neighbours so as to minimize violence and destruction.

The well known philosopher, Bertrand Russell, commented on this issue:

Not long ago, private disputes were often settled by duels, and those who upheld duelling maintained that its abolition would be contrary to human nature. They forgot, as present upholders of war forget, that what is called 'human nature' is, in the main, the result of custom and tradition and education, and, in civilized men, only a very tiny fraction is due to primitive instinct. If the world could live for a few generations without war, war would soon come to seem as absurd as duelling has come to seem to us. No doubt there would still be some homicidal maniacs, but they would no longer be heads of governments.[21]

This all suggests that human nature is much more complex than is implied either by the pessimism of Christianity and modern materialism or by the optimism of the French Enlightenment. A more realistic view, suggested by the evidence of history, is that there are two sides to human nature. On the one hand, there is the 'animal' aspect which springs from the physical need for food, shelter and clothing and from the innate drive to propagate the species. When moderate and under control, this necessary aspect of human nature serves humanity well. However, when it becomes extreme or obsessive, then the result is greed, hatred, and violence. On the other hand, there is the spiritual aspect of human nature which distinguishes humanity from other forms of life: a deep urge to seek the transcendental through religion or art, to love and to give to others, and to cultivate the nobler qualities of character. It is this aspect of human nature which brings the deepest and most long-lasting happiness and sense of fulfilment. When the animal side of our nature dominates, society sinks into barbarism; when the spiritual side is cultivated, civilization soars to heights not attainable at other times.

Understanding of the existence of the two sides of human nature is beginning to emerge in the feminist movement; it is also fundamental to the teachings of the Bahá'í Faith.[22] With such a perspective, the approach to international peace takes on a new meaning. The vision of what might be shines ahead, but at the same time there is an altertness to the dangers of the negative side of international relations. It is possible to respond positively to friendly moves by other nations without being obsessed with the fear that everything must be a trick to gain an advantage. How the peace movement can foster such a change in governmental attitudes is outlined by Lynn Miller in *Global Order*:

Our general goal should be to discourage the

perception of one's opponents as unalterably malign, since perceptions demonstrably produce self-fulfilling prophecies that themselves help maintain instability. That goal can be advanced through a host of actions, all initiated on the premise that my state's positive or benign behavior should serve as an example for the other to emulate. If that emulation does not follow, my government is free to return to its previous policy with little risk to itself.[23]

The Question of Sovereignty

A second major block to rational conduct of international relations, which is just as important as the prevailing negative assessments of human nature, is the view that the absolute sovereignty of the national state is an unchanging law of politics. That being a widely held view, it is considered a waste of time, or downright naive, to raise questions as to whether the international anarchy which automatically flows from such an arrangement is in the best interests of humanity.

All levels of government below the national level – village, city, county, province, state, etc. – recognize that it is necessary for the common good that, to some extent, higher levels of the government hierarchy should have a right of intervention in their territories; but the national level of government alone denies any outside body the right to interfere within its territorial jurisdiction. (It is worth observing, however, that this claim of sovereignty is not always taken to an extreme when facing inwards towards the lower levels of government within its territory. Thus where there is a

31

federal constitution, such local levels of government have independent power and may severely restrict the authority of the national government in their territory.) The claim of sovereignty vis-à-vis foreign states may lead a nation to take unilateral armed action in such cases as disputed territory (e.g. the German attack on Poland in 1939) or alleged oppression of its people in another state (e.g. the German threats against Czechoslovakia in 1938). In other words, the sovereign state acts in a manner which it would never tolerate from its citizens or from any lower level of government; nor will it readily embrace optimum cooperative arrangements with other nations, out of fear that they could lead to loss of sovereignty. Of course there are exceptions to the rule, for instance the founding of the League of Nations, the United Nations and the European Community – but these came into being only after the traumas of the two world wars. The reality is that the cost of national sovereignty for the people concerned can be very high and the benefits small.

The situation is made worse because nations rarely practice symmetry in their approach to the principle of national sovereignty. They will use this principle to justify silence when another nation (especially an ally) exploits or otherwise abuses its own people. However, such scruples are easily put aside if interference is considered useful for immediate self-interest. The temptation to meddle in the affairs of other nations, especially if they are weaker, seems to be very widespread and to be, in effect, part of what is meant by national sovereignty, though few would admit this openly. Clearly, it is a practice which multiplies severalfold the risk of suspicion, hostility and violent conflict between nations. The more powerful a nation is, the more likely it is that it will engage in such activities –

and, as might be expected, the two superpowers are among the worst offenders. For long the United States has asserted its right to interfere in the affairs of other nations in the Americas in order to promote various sectional interests. Rarely, if at all, are vital aspects of US territorial integrity and security involved, nor is it apparent that such interventions have served the interests of the people of the United States well, let alone those of its neighbours. It would be salutary if some independent body were to publish an objective cost/benefit analysis of such exercises in power play. Similarly, Russia practises the right to intervene, with an invading army on occasion, in the affairs of its neighbours in Eastern Europe and along its southern frontier in Asia. It is claimed that such interventions are vital to national security, but the circumstances suggest this argument has been greatly exaggerated. Being superpowers, these two nations do not confine their sovereign rights of intervention in other countries to their immediate neighbours; on the contrary, they will on occasion intervene anywhere in the world if they see some short-term advantage to be gained.

As the power claimed and wielded by the national state is clearly becoming an increasing menace to the welfare of humanity, it is not unreasonable to inquire what is its source. The answer that no doubt will be given is that economies of scale push power to the highest sustainable level of government, and the national level is the highest which can win and maintain deep support from its citizens. This analysis, however, points to a flaw in the view that it is an unchanging law of politics that absolute sovereignty is the unique prerogative of national governments, simply because the nation-state is a comparatively recent creation. In prehistory and for most of recorded history, the natural organizational units of humanity have been the family and the tribe, from which there emerged on occasion the city-state. There have been, of course, much larger political units at various times – such as the military empire and power blocs cobbled together on the basis of regal dynastic marriages – but such organizations have not won lasting and deeply felt loyalty from their polyglot subjects and have tended to collapse, often almost overnight.

The idea that the state should bring together all people of a common culture and language was promulgated by Muḥammad in the seventh century AD, but it was a principle that was not really put into practice by his followers. There are a few isolated early examples of national states in succeeding centuries, usually where people were forced together by geography (e.g. the near-island nation of the British) or by the struggle to overthrow outside oppressors (e.g. the Dutch and the Swiss). It was not until the coming of the French Revolution, with its passionate advocacy of the will of the people, that the idea of nationhood began to capture the imagination of the world. In 1800 there was no more than a handful of independent states that could be described as nations. Today, less than two hundred years later, the vast majority of the 170 or so sovereign states now existing are nations and only a small minority of the world's five billion people live in states that do not represent their nation.

There are two points to note here. The first is that because politics was for so long free of the dominance of the sovereign national state there is good reason for arguing that the present system will not be a permanent feature of future world affairs. The second is that nation-building, which has been one of the dominating themes of the modern age, is now virtually over. Some

34

important changes will have to be made to accommodate peoples still striving for national self-determination or liberty such as the blacks of South Africa, the Armenians, the Basques, the Kurds, the Palestinians and the Sikhs, but compared with the far-reaching changes of the last two centuries such adjustments are relatively minor. That being so, there is a need to start focusing on the next phase in the evolution of human society and not to remain obsessed with human drives that have been all but accommodated.

Some clues as to the character of that new phase have already been given in the events of the last century – particularly those of the last fifty years, running parallel with the final stages of nation-building. There has been a growing number of worldwide forces which are now significantly affecting the everyday lives of ordinary men and women, but which are outside the control of any individual national government, even the most powerful. Such forces include international trade, the international flow of capital and technology, man-made changes in the environment (e.g. the pollution of the Mediterranean Sea and the pollution of Scandinavian skies by European industry), changing cultural standards affecting health and social structures (e.g. drugs and sexual mores), international terrorism and, above all, the threat of nuclear war which would result in disaster both for nations involved and bystanders alike. In other words, whether they like it or not, national governments are finding that their precious sovereignty is being eroded; and in order to regain some control over their destinies, they are being forced by events to cooperate – hence the United Nations and a multiplicity of other international organizations.

A wide variety of studies makes it clear that such trends will continue and if anything become more intense and urgent. The record shows that when political institutions bend to the winds of history, society flourishes (e.g. Britain in the nineteenth century); and when they oppose them, there is confusion and disaster (e.g. the Tsarist regime in Russia). Thus in the present situation, when international cooperation is becoming such a vital necessity for the well-being of all, the old political nostrums modelled on the writings of Machiavelli or the actions of Bismarck that used to sound so sophisticated and worldly wise are now increasingly irrelevant and counterproductive to the interests of all nations. Those with an international perspective must turn around popular misconceptions and assert loudly and clearly that they are the practical realists, and that it is the traditional self-serving and blinkered nationalists who are dreamers out of touch with reality.

Perhaps a useful way of illuminating the condition of humanity today is to picture it in terms of an individual who has lived through the cycle of infancy and childhood and just experienced, through the democratic, national and scientific revolutions of the last two centuries, the turbulence of adolescence. The aptness of this metaphor is illustrated by H. B. Danesh in *Unity: The Creative Foundation of Peace*:

The adolescent mentality of humanity during the twentieth century has been so dominant that we have collectively adopted it, consequently viewing both our lives and our world from an unhealthy adolescent perspective. Our music, clothes, food, hobbies, work habits, sexual orientation, personal ambitions, and value systems are, to a very large degree, those of an adolescent, and we are so immersed in this mentality that we have lost our objectivity.[24]

Humanity has now reached the point in life where it has to start using the education and physical power gained in those years of adolescence in a rational manner for its own good. The division and violence of adolescence has to give way to the cooperation and unity of adulthood.

Once it is recognized that we are entering into a new age in which the nation-state will no longer be sovereign, then it becomes easier to start changing priorities in diplomacy and international relations. Instead of immediately asking in every situation 'What is in this for us (the national government) right now?', the question will become 'What are the underlying implications here for the welfare not only of our own people, but also of all other peoples?' – because, if for no other reason, it is acknowledged that the latter has great bearing on the former.

In making such a change in the priorities of diplomacy, there is obviously a critical role to be played by the two superpowers. Their influence and power of example is crucial. If they continue to act in a lawless and irresponsible way, then there will always be other governments looking for an excuse for irresponsible behaviour who will follow their example. The point to stress here is that the record of the two superpowers is very far from being completely unprincipled. Both have an enlightened and visionary side to their diplomacy. Thus the USA, true to the spirit of Jefferson and Lincoln, played a major role in the creation of the World Court, the League of Nations and the United Nations and in the drafting of the Universal Declaration of Human Rights. Russia too has taken important initiatives of a similar nature, playing a leading role in the establishment of the Congress sytem in nineteenth-century Europe and the convening of the Hague peace conferences and proposing radical approaches to disarmament in the decades since World War II. The superpowers should take pride in this enlightened record and use it as a springboard for future policy. Above all, they must uphold international law and order (including the World Court), assist in the elimination of world poverty and uphold the principles enshrined in the Universal Declaration of Human Rights.

Of course, all cannot be left to the two superpowers; there is an important role to be played by each of the other 170 or so independent states. Indeed, a number of important states (China, India, Japan, West Germany, France, Great Britain, Italy, Brazil and Indonesia) have responsibilities similar to those of the superpowers, though on a lesser scale. Third World countries, being a majority and representing a majority of the world's population, have a particular responsibility in setting an example of enlightened foreign policy. They could easily put aside the routine confrontational rhetoric at the United Nations which brings all concerned into disrepute. Instead, they could take the initiative by helping mediate disputes between others, set an example by using international tribunals for even the most critical issues and act according to conscience when human rights violations are brought to the United Nations. In particular, much is to be expected of those countries which lay claim to respect as free, democratic, and progressive societies. It is encouraging that some nations (among them Canada, Costa Rica, the Netherlands, Switzerland and the Scandinavian countries) have already given enlightened leadership in developing internationally-oriented foreign policies. The media would serve humanity well if they were to focus more attention on such positive developments rather than always concentrating on the negative aspects of diplomacy.

The Unity of Mankind

The third major obstacle standing in the path leading to the elimination of the main causes of war and to the establishment of world peace is resistance to the idea of the unity of mankind. As noted in the last section, for many people the highest level of social loyalty is to the nation – and while that remains the case, there will continue to be such resistance to cooperation between nations and to the peaceful solution of mutual difficulties.

The concept of the unity of mankind is closely linked to the historical forces which shape international relations today. It is an immensely powerful concept which adds an emotional dimension to the intellectual case for international cooperation and unity. It is an idea which has been central to the teachings of all the great religions,[25] and it is a significant aspect of humanism, that secular offshoot of Western religious traditions. The reality of moral exhortation has been confirmed by recent experience. Science has shown that very nearly all the characteristics of the physical body are common to all human beings and that differences on account of race are extremely minor. Old adages that some races are inherently more intelligent than others have been shown to be totally false by such evidence as cultural groups progressing from an IQ well below average to one well above average in the space of two generations. International trade and travel, migration, the transistor radio, mass circulation newspapers and television, all manifestations of modern civilization, have served to bring peoples of all nations and backgrounds into closer contact with one another. In the short run, the process has at times caused friction and perhaps a heightened sense of difference, but in the longer term the result will be a growing understanding that all people have the same human spirit and that none of us can be free so long as any are oppressed or deprived of the basic necessities of life.

That human suffering touches us all is poignantly expressed by the famous lines from John Donne's *Devotions*, written in 1624:

Any man's death diminishes me, because I am involved in Mankinde; And therefore never send to know for whom the bell tolls; It tolls for thee.

The same is of course no less true today: a picture of a starving child evokes a response in the breast of every man and woman, regardless of race, nation or class. Such feelings must not be crushed by the daily flow of talk about 'megatonnage', 'body counts' and other dehumanized jargon or by the propaganda of terrorism, for a deep sense of the unity of mankind is the only base on which lasting peace can be built.

Clearly, one important way to nurture a sense of the unity of mankind is through education. It has long been recognized that education is the key to economic and social development and is therefore an important tool in removing one of the main causes of war: extremes of wealth and poverty. But in the interests of peace, education needs to be taken much further. All citizens, children and adults alike, should have access to material which not only encourages pride in their own culture but an appreciation of the beauty and diversity of the culture of all other peoples. Furthermore, children should not be taught to glorify war or the conquest of other peoples. A common language is one of the strongest cultural instruments for unifying a nation and in the long run it is obvious that one of the key roles of education for removing barriers between peoples will be the teaching of an auxiliary world language, an idea associated with both the Bahá'í Faith and the name of Ludovic Zamenhof (1858–1917), creator of the international language Esperanto. Already the use of a certain 'lingua franca' for international trade and communities, most notably English in the twentieth century, has demonstrated some of the benefits that could be obtained from a true world auxiliary language.

The logic of historical trends and the concept of the unity of mankind lead inevitably to the idea of world government. This idea raises such fears in some people, so they say, that they seem to prefer the risk of nuclear devastation. The reasons for such fears are numerous and complex and there is little space to analyse them here, but a good account of them can be found in Chapter II of *World Peace and World Government* by J. Tyson (see Bibliography). One of the greatest fears is that a world government would be dictatorial, simply because it would possess a unique monopoly of supreme power, and that it might be heavily influenced by authoritarian nations. Today the majority of the 170 independent states of the world, including some of the most powerful and populous, are indeed ruled by authoritarian governments; and so long as that remains the case, the prospect of a world government remains dim.

However, there is good reason to believe that there is a historical trend against authoritarianism, a welcome

41

sign of the maturing of civilization. Complex economies, educated societies, the information explosion, are all forces which tend to make authoritarian government ineffective and open society more likely. Moreover, the experience of voluntary federations both at national and regional levels (such as the United States, Australia and the European Community) indicates that constitutions can be so devised as to preclude excessive central power – for example, by separation of powers between the executive, legislative and judicial functions and by retention of local powers by the federal units.

In fact, the real danger is that a world government would not be given sufficient power to carry out its functions, as happened both with the League of Nations and with the United Nations. Quite apart from constitutional safeguards, a world government bent on dictatorship would almost certainly have difficulty commanding the loyalty of its own staff and it would also have to face the opposition of a large number of nations. Even today the superpowers, despite all their military paraphernalia, have found it difficult to effectively dominate nations as small as Vietnam and Afghanistan. In a demilitarized and educated world the prospect of a maverick world government seeking to dictate to the rest of humanity seems very remote indeed – and certainly far more remote than the risk of nuclear war under the existing political system.

Although it is unlikely that a true world government will be established in the near future, it is the logical outcome of present long-term trends and would provide many benefits. It should therefore be seen as a main feature of the long-term scenario used by ordinary citizens and diplomats alike when planning and managing present-day international relations.

Long-Term Objectives

Perhaps the easiest and best approach to building world peace is to work forward logically from the situation where humanity finds itself today, thus keeping firmly in touch with current reality and at the same time suggesting how we might get from here to there. As noted earlier, even if the present disarmament negotiations between the superpowers are fruitful, there will still remain thousands of nuclear weapons in the hands of each superpower. Many regard this as a desirable objective in a dangerous world. However, it has to be recognized that it would still leave humanity exposed to the risk of a nuclear holocaust by accident, miscalculation or the deliberate action of madmen. This would be a fragile peace, not all that great an advance over the situation today, and at an early stage the superpowers would have to face the issue of complete nuclear disarmament. But that in turn would create three further problems.

First, there would have to be extreme precautions – including a comprehensive nuclear test ban treaty, covering underground as well as atmospheric explosions, and universal monitoring and inspection so as to make sure that neither superpower gained military advantage by secretly cheating. Secondly, such treaties would have to apply to other nuclear powers, otherwise those nations would have an advantage denied to the superpowers. Thirdly, there would be the risk that the removal of nuclear weapons would increase the likelihood of conventional war between the superpowers and their allies. Indeed, the West has always maintained that it developed nuclear weapons as a deterrent against attack, particularly in Europe, by the larger conventional forces of the Warsaw Pact. Accordingly,

43

there would be a need for a major reduction in the conventional forces of both sides. It would not be sufficient simply to achieve parity: if the superpowers retained large conventional forces, there would remain a major risk because, as demonstrated in France in 1940, a skilfully directed force can attack and destroy another force of the same size. Only reduction to a minimum would preclude such a possibility.

However, here is yet another difficulty: the superpowers will never agree to such drastic reduction in their conventional forces while the forces of other nations remain untouched. In other words, reduction of the conventional forces of the superpowers would almost certainly require similar actions by all other nations.

Attractive though the prospect of worldwide disarmament is, it has to be recognized that even such a desirable step towards peace would only be a first move and that peace will still remain unstable so long as large sections of the world's population continue to have deep grievances and there continues to be a widespread sense of injustice. Disarmament will therefore have to be accompanied by workable procedures for handling national grievances and disputes. This will mean long-term commitment to the eradication of all the causes of war discussed earlier. Ultimately, lasting peace will only be feasible in a world where every man, woman and child has an opportunity to develop his or her full potential not only physically but mentally and spiritually, too. The question then arises as to whether such an objective can be reached without a profound spiritual renaissance and the adoption by the vast majority of humanity, including those holding public office, of new and advanced ethical values.

The logical connection between these stages of development does not mean, of course, that the stages have to follow one another in the order described above. Clearly many of the stages could and should evolve in parallel; however, the urgency of the situation does suggest some parameters to sequence. For instance, it is not reasonable to argue, as some do, that no progress can be made until the whole of humanity has undergone a spiritual reawakening, vital as that is to the long-term interests of peace. Such a development is not likely to happen overnight – and meanwhile we live with the constant danger of a nuclear holocaust. We must indeed work as hard as possible for such a spiritual renaissance, for which millions around the world sense a need at the personal as well as the community level; but at the same time we must grapple with the technical problems of diplomacy and disarmament. It is vital that the two processes go forward hand in hand.

PART TWO

A Blueprint for Peace

CHAPTER 3

Twelve Proposals for World Peace

It is perhaps useful to introduce this chapter with three preliminary observations. First, the proposals set out below have universal application and are not confined to relationships between the two superpowers. Clearly, relations between the two superpowers are a critical factor in the peace process if for no other reason than that they own between them some 90 per cent of all nuclear weapons and their expenditures on military affairs represent about 60 per cent of the world total (see Appendix II). Furthermore, they have a major influence on the actions of other nations. Nevertheless, as discussed in the previous chapter, the logic of the peace process shows that other nations have to be equally committed. After all, most of the wars being waged in the world today do not directly involve the superpowers.

Secondly, though the approach is universal, the proposals made are primarily concerned with the first steps along the path to peace. There is no attempt to outline a comprehensive plan covering the whole process through to the establishment of a lasting peace based on justice and a sense of universal brotherhood, which may take many decades or even one or two centuries to achieve. As the proposals are only the first steps, it is not unreasonable to discuss implementation in terms of a specific timetable. The purpose of suggesting such a timetable is that it serves to focus the mind on the issue and reinforce the idea of peace as the first priority. The year chosen, 2000 AD, is a significant date in the calendar most universally used, and therefore one that can capture the imagination. With peace as the highest priority, there is no reason why this goal should not be achieved.

Thirdly, the suggestions made here are to a large extent based on ideas which have been discussed on and off for decades, especially in connection with the founding of the League of Nations and the United Nations, and on lessons learned from those discussions. It is hoped that, taken together, they may amount to more than the sum of their parts.

1 A World Peace Constituency

During the United Nations International Year of Peace, various peace organizations and movements around the world succeeded in raising consciousness about peace issues among large numbers of people. It is vital that this forward impetus should not be lost: with thoughtful direction these movements have the potential to exercise a critical influence on the policies of the nations of the world. The following two suggestions are made with this in mind.

A practical peace programme   If the peace movement is to be really effective, it must come forward with a practical programme, possibly along the lines suggested in this book, which can be accepted by the vast majority of people. As Einstein put it, one factor that would 'make war a virtual impossibility is the existence of a united public opinion in all important countries . . . so powerful that all governments would be compelled to renounce a measure of their sovereignty.'[26] This means, on the one hand, a programme based on *key global principles* that apply equally to all nations. On the other hand, it means the abandonment of confrontational tactics and a preoccupation with divisive local issues. These issues, such as variations on the theme of unilateral disarmament, arouse intense opposition because they lack evenhandedness. They therefore create disunity and ineffectiveness. Global principles must be adopted because this is the only approach which is likely to be acceptable in countries with authoritarian governments. The peace movement must extend to all nations: if it is confined to the so-called 'open societies', it loses much of its credibility and potential effectiveness.

Furthermore, to make the peace process viable, detailed specialist knowledge will be required on a wide range of related subjects. The peace movement needs the support of all manner of experts such as physicists, environmentalists, doctors, economists, sociologists, statesmen, etc. Associations of such experts have already made some of the most valuable contributions to the peace process. Their continued effective support is most likely if the peace movement demonstrates a sense of responsibility and intellectual integrity to match its idealism. It is also very important to involve military personnel in the process and not to take the attitude that they are all warmongers. Many soldiers are convinced that in their professional capacity they are also contributing to the maintenance of peace, and the peace movement needs their expert advice and support. The advice of soldiers may be particularly important with regard to the characteristics of weapons and many of the technical aspects of switching from an offensive based strategy to one of defence (see Section 4 below).

This is not to suggest that the peace movement should become cold and intellectual. There is a need too for the popular expression of emotion and the human spirit in public demonstrations, etc. However, care should be taken to ensure that such events really do convey the spirit of peace and that they are joyous occasions which will attract people of all backgrounds. This might be done by putting an emphasis on a role for young children, using symbols such as candles and flowers, and by making provision not only for pop groups to lead the crowds in songs of brotherhood but also for the saying of prayers for peace.

A world federation of peace movements A second requirement is that the peace movement become truly global and establish branches in every nation of the world, which should then join together in a worldwide federation. It is essential for the movement to maintain unity, for if it should fall to quarrelling it will have no credibility at all. The peace movement needs to mobilize popular sentiment, to create a real 'peace constituency', which will persuade politicians in democratic and authoritarian nations alike that peace should have the highest priority. The importance of harnessing the persuasive power of public opinion is stressed by Lynn Miller in *Global Order*:

The relevant decision-makers within governments almost certainly cannot be expected to play the disarmament game seriously until they are pushed into doing so – and pushed by the conviction that

52

it is far too important to our security to be treated as a game.[27]

2 A World Peace Assembly

An expanded peace constituency could propose to the leaders of the nations that they convoke a world assembly dedicated exclusively to the issue of peace. It is hard to envisage on what grounds this could be opposed – for, as Benjamin Ferencz argues in *A Commonsense Guide to World Peace*, 'there is no country on earth that would dare to oppose peace as an objective of government.'[28]

Of course there have been many world conferences which have been slow to convene and ever slower to take action – e.g. the disarmament conferences of the thirties and the current efforts to achieve peace in the Middle East and South East Asia. To avoid such difficulties, the proposed conference should have the strong backing of a worldwide and united peace constituency and an agenda with the single objective of peace as its highest priority.

The suggestion made here is that the agenda of such a peace assembly should include seven interrelated draft treaties designed to bring about the end of war. It might also discuss a programme of supplementary measures which would reinforce the treaties. The proposed treaties and supplementary measures are discussed in the following paragraphs. Before the proposed peace assembly meets, it might be appropriate to circulate a standard peace questionnaire to the governments of all the members of the United Nations in order to elicit their views on key peace issues. The questionnaire might also be used to poll the general public around the world, as well as various professional organizations, special interest groups, etc. A possible draft for such a questionnaire is shown in Appendix III.

3 A Treaty to Outlaw War Between Nations

Moral and legal significance A formal statement outlawing war and ratified by all nations is necessary to make clear, once and for all, that in the view of the peoples of the world war is no longer an acceptable method of conducting international relations and that it is a crime against all humanity. Whatever may have been the arguments in the past in favour of war as sometimes the only means of removing an injustice, it is now clear that in the nuclear age all wars involve a risk so great that it dwarfs any possible gain. There should be no exceptions: no arguments for 'just wars', no vague equivocations about an 'inherent right' to self-defence that might be used to justify aggression. Such a declaration by all the nations of the world would have great moral significance and provide a legal basis for action against any aggressor nation.

International and national measures of support Of course, it would be possible for governments to make such a declaration and carry on as usual, as happened after the signing of the Kellogg–Briand Pact of 1928 (see Appendix I). To make a treaty renouncing war effective it would have to be linked to six other treaties proposing the abolition of all offensive weapons by all nations; a programme of sanctions to be taken against any nation that engages in war; the compulsory arbitration of international disputes; the election of a World Peace Council; the establishment of an international police force; and the creation of an independent peace fund for the

United Nations. In addition, it would be highly desirable for such an international treaty outlawing war to be supplemented by national legislation in as many countries as possible. Such legislation could take the form of amendments to national constitutions, or free-standing laws which would require the removal and prosecution of members of any executive branch of government which started a war against another nation. The seriousness of such matters needs to be impressed on governments at every opportunity.

A definition of war An important aspect of such a treaty would be the definition of war. So far the United Nations has been content with a very general statement, approved by the General Assembly in 1974, defining war as:

> . . . the use of armed force by a state against the sovereignty, territorial integrity or political independence of another state, or in any other manner inconsistent with the Charter of the United Nations.

A more precise and operational definition would have to be devised by lawyers with a mandate to apply their skills to the resolution of complex problems, rather than to complicating them further. However, there are some broad points which are clear. War is when one country kills a large number of another country's citizens and destroys their land and property; war is when a country is invaded and occupied by another, either in part or completely; war is when a country is subjected to a blockade intended to starve its people and destroy its economy. In recent years there have been two further variants, which are somewhat more difficult to define in precise terms. The first is the situation of guerilla warfare, in which one nation provides support to an armed rebellion inside another country. The second is the attempt by one nation to put pressure on another nation or the community of nations by (often secretly) sponsoring international terrorism outside its own borders, as in the case of hijackings and attacks on airlines and airports. It is more difficult to identify the aggressor nations engaged in these forms of war, but the effort has to be made lest other nations waver in their commitment to the abolition of orthodox forms of warfare.

4 A Treaty to Abolish all Offensive Weapons

The current debate The recent public debate on disarmament has produced a wide range of options. With regard to nuclear weapons, suggestions have been made to freeze the number of weapons at present levels; to abolish certain types of weapons (for example, intermediate range weapons, as in the INF Treaty, or battlefield weapons); to 'build down' stocks; to make 'deep cuts'; to halve the number of strategic weapons (as in START); and to reduce numbers to the minimum needed for deterrence (say 1,000 each for the USA and USSR, compared with about 25,000 each today). There is even talk of complete nuclear disarmament. With regard to conventional arms, negotiations for major reductions in the forces of NATO and the Warsaw Pact in Central Europe have been going on for years; and thought is now being given to extending the scenario to cover all of Europe (excluding neutrals) west of the Ural mountains.

The problem with half-measures Though there may

be merit in each of these approaches, in so far as agreement on any one of them might reduce tension between the superpowers, at least temporarily, none of them completely removes the danger of war. There is always the risk of nuclear conflicts so long as nuclear weapons are available to nations. Futhermore, a major cut or abolition of nuclear weapons may increase the risk of conventional war. As noted earlier, Western nations originally justified such weapons as a balance or deterrent to the larger conventional forces of Russia and her allies in Europe. Reductions in conventional forces in Europe also present problems. First, during a crisis Russia would always be able to reinforce her troops in Eastern Europe quickly, whereas the USA would have to bring in reinforcements for her troops in Western Europe from across the Atlantic. Secondly, numerical superiority alone is not necessarily a deterrent: there is always the risk of an attack or invasion by a conventional force that is better trained or more skilfully led, and factors such as geography or surprise can create a tactical advantage. Yet a third weakness is that the public debate on disarmament is almost solely concerned with the two superpowers and, to a lesser extent, their main allies: yet clearly there is a limit to the degree of disarmament these powers will contemplate so long as the rest of the world remains fully armed.

A radical approach These considerations make necessary a radical approach involving (i) abolition of all offensive weapons and (ii) a universal application to all nations. The failure of radical approaches to disarmament in the past – for example, the Disarmament Conference of the League of Nations in the early 1930s, the Soviet proposal for complete disarmament in 1945 and the McCloy–Zonin discussions of the early 1960s – might prompt scepticism towards such a proposal. One response to such criticism is that the proposal made here differs from those discussed earlier in so far as it is part of an integrated package that will provide safeguards against concerns which in the past have always stopped the radical approach. Another is that a radical approach has the great advantage of cutting through the dense undergrowth of technical argument that typically slows negotiations to a virtual standstill – such as weapons counts, weapon equivalents, diverse strategic and tactical considerations, and wrangling over which nations should be included. Thirdly, it has the advantage from the ethical point of view that it proposes a peace based on defence rather than offensive considerations. This moral argument should not be lightly dismissed, since it is one which will tend to strengthen public support everywhere and thereby make cheating more difficult.

Distinguishing between offensive and defensive weapons   One of the greatest impediments to progress in disarmament discussions has been the failure to draw the crucial distinction between offensive and defensive weapons. There have been two main reasons for this. One has been the straightforward view that it is not possible to distinguish offensive from defensive weapons. There was always something unpersuasive about this argument. It may have had more validity during the interwar disarmament discussions than it does today, if only because military manpower, which is largely dual purpose, weighed more heavily in the relative balance of power. But whatever the situation may have been in the past, it is clear that today most weapons can be divided into those that are essentially either offensive or defensive (see below). Furthermore, those weapons that are essentially defensive are inefficient when used offensively, and therefore do not represent a serious threat to peace. The other main reason attention has not been focused on the abolition of offensive weapons is the all too seductive argument that attack is the best means of defence. Perhaps this view has some validity when taken in isolation. However, it no longer has any when seen in the broader context of a comprehensive approach that includes provisions for inspection for compliance as well as universal sanctions against a state which goes to war. This distinction between offensive and defensive weaponry is of great importance, and the complete abolition of offensive weapons *without exception* would be a decisive factor in reducing tensions. It would strongly discourage aggression because it would be clear in advance that an armed attack on other nations using defensive weapons would be difficult, and would almost certainly not lead to any useful advantage for the aggressor nation.

Offensive weapons In view of the above, the first element of this proposal, with regard to disarmament, is that all the nations of the world simultaneously destroy all their offensive weapons and agree not to replace them. Offensive weapons would be defined in the first instance as devices for mass destruction, such as nuclear bombs and chemical and biological weapons. (This policy would obviously also require an end to all testing of nuclear weapons.) In the second instance, they would include all vehicles for the delivery of such devices: ballistic missiles, pilotless flying bombs, first-line military aircraft (including both bombers and fighters), heavy artillery, aircraft-carriers, as well as submarines and surface ships equipped with bombardment missiles and large calibre guns. In addition there are the so-called conventional offensive weapons such as heavy tanks and torpedo-carrying submarines. Failure to include such conventional weapons in the category to be abolished would mean that nations were treated unequally, and there would remain a real risk of aggressive military action by nations given the advantage.

Defensive weapons The second element of the proposal, balancing the first, is that all countries should be allowed to maintain as many defensive weapons as they feel are needed to protect themselves against a sneak attack by a nation cheating on disarmament. Such weapons would include anti-missile, anti-aircraft, anti-tank, anti-submarine and anti-mine systems, as well as fixed fortifications within the home territory. Anti-missile systems are the one kind of 'defensive' weapon that presents a potentially serious offensive threat, in so far as they may have the capacity to destroy spy satellites and thereby eliminate an essential element in the defences of another power. To obviate this possibility, it is proposed that:

i) all spy satellites be made United Nations property and be administered by United Nations personnel;

ii) each satellite should survey both superpowers;

iii) each satellite should have two sections, one for each superpower. However, the design would have to ensure that if one part were knocked out, the other part would also cease to function.

Regular and military forces Nations should be encouraged to reduce their regular armed forces to a minimum and to rely for defence on the system least threatening to others, which is a militia capable of being mobilized in an emergency to defend the territory on a local basis. (A possible model might be the system used successfully by Switzerland for many decades.) In other words, countries should be encouraged to make themselves into defensive 'hedgehogs' that are very costly and painful to attack. Countries should also be permitted to retain sufficient forces to maintain internal law and order, including the capability to suppress internal insurrection. Such forces might require some light attack planes, light tanks or armoured cars and light artillery. With the focus of attention switched from offence to defence, governments could perhaps pay more attention to the very real potential threat of sneak attacks by unorthodox means, such as nuclear weapons smuggled in aboard a visiting merchant ship. Initially countries deprived of their familiar armoury might feel a need for a rather extensive 'security blanket' of defensive forces, but a prolonged period of peace would undoubtedly encourage a radical reduction in the burden of defence spending.

Reversal of orthodox views The above approach is, of course, the direct opposite of the orthodox theory of peace through fear, or 'Mutually Assured Destruction' (MAD). One aspect of MAD is that it treats offensive weapons as no more dangerous than defensive weapons, such as anti-ballistic missile systems. Such a lunatic philosophy creates cynicism, because it contravenes both morality and common sense. Its major flaw is that it depends on all nuclear powers acting rationally all the time. As the years go by, the odds against such good fortune are bound to lengthen. This is one of many instances of the lack of clear thinking which is induced by a political system based on the sovereign national state.

Dismantling military alliances The abolition of offensive weapons and the introduction of hedgehog-style defence systems would logically require the dismantling of all existing military alliances and the withdrawal of all foreign troops and military bases from every country. NATO and the Warsaw Pact would be disbanded; American forces in Europe would retire across the Atlantic, and Soviet forces behind the Russian–Polish frontier. Western Europe would be protected because the USSR would not have the offensive weapons required for aggressive action, and there would be advance warning of an attack because its forces would have to cross several Eastern European countries in order to reach the West. Furthermore, it might be expected that the Eastern European countries would not take kindly to Soviet troops entering their territory for such purposes once they had been with-drawn. The USSR and Eastern Europe would be secure from Western attack on the same basis.

Confidence-building in Europe In this context it cannot be stressed too strongly that both sides in the European confrontation since 1945 have had good reason for fear and a sense of insecurity: to achieve peace every effort has to be made to provide mutual reassurance of safety. On the one hand Russia has suffered three major invasions from the West since 1800: in the Napoleonic Wars and World Wars I and II. The Crimean War might be considered a fourth. On the other hand, the USSR has acquired dominance in

Eastern Europe by military force and for forty years has kept in place a preponderant ground force, complete with mass tank formations and other offensive armaments which cannot but arouse fears in the West. In view of this near paranoic situation it might be advisable not to proceed with the dismantling of alliances immediately. The abolition of alliances, though a logical sequence to the destruction of all offensive weapons, is not essential, and in consequence they could be phased out over a decade or two as mutual fears subside.

Third-party military barriers In view of the deep suspicions existing between mutually hostile nations, it might be necessary to provide additional reassurance to the parties concerned by the insertion, at least for a transitional period, of an international force between the two sides. In Europe this could be done along the Polish–Russian border and the border between East and West Germany, where international forces would act as a 'trip wire' defence against attack by either side. Similar arrangements might also be necessary in other tense areas of the world – for example, between Israel and her neighbours, India and Pakistan, the two Koreas, etc. Such forces should be large enough to guard key communications points but not strong enough to threaten anyone, and they should be drawn from third-party nations trusted by both sides.

Monitoring disarmament Of course, the successful abolition of all offensive weapons would depend very much on monitoring teams being allowed to enter every country to supervise the destruction of existing stocks. The monitoring teams would have to be placed in factories and military bases to make sure that old weapons were not replaced with new ones, and would preferably be manned by personnel from third-party countries under the aegis of the United Nations. However, it would have to be assumed, at least initially, that many nations, including the superpowers, would want to have their own representatives on monitoring teams in countries with which they are in dispute. The major advance in verification procedures incorporated in the INF treaty and the recent experience of both superpowers with on-site monitoring of each other's underground nuclear tests suggest that this need not be a critical problem.

The possibility of cheating   Nevertheless, it should be assumed as a matter of prudence that no monitoring system is likely to be completely foolproof, and that a determined aggressor will be able to build offensive weapons in secret. However, an effective monitoring system would undoubtedly make this difficult, and would certainly preclude the deployment of large numbers of such weapons. In addition, the proposed comprehensive ban on the testing of nuclear weapons would make it virtually impossible to develop or even maintain such weapons in the long run. Tests, which are relatively easy to detect even when underground, are becoming increasingly more important for nuclear weapons development. As Robert McNamara points out in *Blundering into Disaster*:

[While] in the past only about six nuclear tests were required to develop a weapon, perfecting one of the new more complex designs we are working on today will require at least one hundred to two hundred explosions . . . The physics we are looking at is far more complicated than anything we have looked at before.[29]

Furthermore, existing weapons begin to deteriorate after two or three decades and become unusable. Accordingly, there should be no risk of a sudden massive and overwhelming attack, as is possible today. Admittedly, small-scale nuclear attacks could occur, in theory at least, but a potential aggressor would be greatly deterred by knowing in advance that hedgehog-type defences would make complete victory unlikely and that the cost of such an attack would be extremely high as a result of massive retaliatory sanctions by all the nations of the world.

5 A Treaty to Apply Universal Sanctions Against Aggressors

Like disarmament, collective security is an area of endeavour littered with failed initiatives, such as those against Italy in the thirties and against Rhodesia in the seventies. The reasons are many, but they surely include the short-term perspective of national interest, consideration of the issue in isolation (i.e. separately from disarmament) and the absence of machinery for enforcement. The suggestions made here are intended to take account of the lessons learned from these experiences.

Non-violent sanctions The first element of the proposal regarding collective security is that the main-stay of enforcement should be non-violent sanctions, both because they are morally preferable and because they are more likely to win voluntary compliance from all the states of the world. In today's international environment the concept of world citizenship is not yet widely accepted, and one nation might well be reluctant to send its soldiers to the other side of the world to be killed in defence of another country with which it has little in common or for which it has little sympathy until all other options have been exhausted. This should not be a cause for despair, because there is in fact a range of non-violent sanctions that could be implemented and would be painful enough to deter all but the most determined of aggressors. Such sanctions could include:

i) an absolute ban on all trade and commercial transactions;

ii) the severing of all communication links such as airlines, railways, road transport, ships, telephones, telegraph, etc.;

iii) the closing down of national embassies and consulates, leaving a representative of the Secretary-General of the United Nations as the only channel of communication with the outside world;

iv) the repatriation of all citizens of the aggressor nation who are abroad, unless they have refugee status.

It would be necessary, in addition, for the international community to make its point of view well known to the citizens of the aggressor country by using every means available, including radio and television broadcasts.

Military sanctions Though the main emphasis should be on non-violent sanctions, there might well be a need for supporting low-intensity military operations too. For instance, it could be necessary to blockade the frontiers of the aggressor nation by land, air and sea. This might eventually lead to the risk that some of the population in the aggressor country would starve. In such cases the United Nations should offer to supply food to the affected areas, but should insist on complete control (i.e. direct distribution under armed guard) so as to prevent the aggressor exploiting the situation, as has often happened in the past.

Another scenario might involve the protective sealing of borders by military forces when a government complains that outsiders are giving military aid to an internal armed rebellion. Yet another possibility is an invasion that involves progressive encroachment after the first attack. In such a case it might be desirable to place an international military force in a blocking position in the line of advance; and if all other means failed, it might even be necessary to counter-attack in order to drive an aggressor from an invaded country. As a matter of principle, no nation should be allowed to retain an advantage gained from aggressive military action. The composition of the international forces needed for enforcing military sanctions is discussed in Section 8 below.

The implementation of sanctions It would be important for sanctions to be applied immediately and in full force as soon as it has been determined that a state of war exists. This determination should be made by a World Peace Council elected by the Security Council of the United Nations. In the case of bombings or invasion the situation would be clear cut. In the case of assistance to internal armed rebellion the situation might be unclear at first if, as is probable, the assistance

67

is covert. In such cases the Council might appoint a flying investigative commission to determine the validity of the complaints made, and sanctions would not be applied until the commission had determined that armed aggression had occurred or was taking place.

The period of sanctions   Sanctions should continue to apply until:

i) the invading forces have been withdrawn;

ii) the aggressor has agreed to pay compensation for damages as determined by the World Court;

iii) the aggressor country has handed over for trial by the World Court those officials who gave the orders to use weapons of mass destruction or to invade the territory of another country. International terrorists and officials responsible for sheltering them should likewise be handed over for trial.

The enforcement of sanctions   Past experience of the application of international sanctions (particularly economic sanctions) has shown that sometimes governments will secretly break their word in order to gain some short-term advantage, as in the case of the UN sanctions against Rhodesia in the 1970s. This possibility could be countered by a system of third-party inspectors, acting under the direction of the United Nations, placed in every country to supervise the application of sanctions. In addition, public opinion in all countries should be mobilized in support of the measures. Any country found to be evading sanctions to a significant degree would be treated as an accomplice of the aggressor and therefore liable to sanctions in turn.

6 A Treaty to Provide for a New World Peace Council

The need for a World Peace Council   The successful application of sanctions will depend to a large extent on nations being confident that the situation has been objectively assessed. Unfortunately, none of the existing United Nations institutions is likely at present to be trusted by all parties to make such an assessment. The Security Council has responsibility for maintaining the peace under the terms of the United Nations Charter; but it is crippled by, among other things, the veto system, which allows a great power to be judge in its own case or in the case of its allies, and it clearly lacks world vision. Even if the veto is abolished, it is unlikely that the Security Council could live down forty years of blatant partisanship and win the confidence of the peoples of the world. The General Assembly is too large and unwieldy for such a task, which may require rapid decision-making, and in any case it too is presently highly fractured and lacking in world vision. The burden of decisions involved is simply too heavy to impose on a single person, and therefore should not be left to the UN Secretary-General.

The World Court has demonstrated better than the other collective institutions of the United Nations that it has a strong global perspective, but its detachment from political power, though useful for judicial functions, would hamper it in deciding on highly political actions such as the identification of a state of war and the sanctions to be applied. For these functions a new body is needed – a World Peace Council, which would combine the political prestige of the Security Council with the objectivity of the World Court.

The functions of a World Peace Council   The primary functions of the Council would concern the application of sanctions against aggressor nations. This would involve deciding:

i) when a state of war exists;

ii) what sanctions should be applied, and when and by whom;

iii) what action should be taken to implement and supervise sanctions;

iv) what nations, if any, are failing to carry out sanctions and what action should be taken against them;

v) when sanctions should be terminated (i.e. after the aggressor has complied with the conditions described in Section 5 above).

In addition, the World Peace Council could act as a Court of Appeal when the World Court has ruled that territory should change hands.

The composition and decision-making structure of the World Peace Council   In order to conform fully with the United Nations Charter and to ensure political prestige, the Peace Council should be elected by the Security Council. The two superpowers should be given an automatic right to membership along with China and India, the other two powers with very large populations. However, it would be necessary to make sure that the Peace Council was structured so as to encourage a truly global perspective. The following suggestions might help achieve this:

1 *Membership* Nine members are proposed, of which four would be from the largest powers in terms of population (one each from the USA, USSR, China and India) and four from the four main continents (one each from Africa, Asia, the Americas and Europe). The members from the continents would not include representatives from the USA, USSR, China and India. Australasia, the continent with the smallest population, could join one of the other four continents for the purpose of electing a member to the Council. To reinforce the global nature of the institution and detach it from identification with individual powers, the ninth position would be filled by a chairperson selected by the other eight.[30]

2 *Elections* There should be at least two nominations for each seat. Nominations would be accepted from 'non-seat areas' as well as from 'seat areas', provided that they were endorsed by the 'seat area' representative on the Security Council; for instance, nominations for the Soviet seat could be made by the Soviet Union and by other members of the Security Council. Election to the eight seats would be by members of the Security Council, each of whom would initially vote for all eight seats at one time. The eight with the highest number of votes for their 'constituencies' would be elected. The purpose of election by the whole Security Council rather than selection by the nations and regions concerned is, of couse, to give the members a degree of independence and freedom to act as world citizens.

3 *Term of office* The term of office should be six years.

However, it would be desirable to have a staggered timetable of elections similar to those for the World Court, so that elections for three seats would take place every two years on a rotating basis. Systems of staggered rotation have the merit of both continuity and gradual change.

4 *Decision-making* Council decisions should be by a two-thirds majority, or a minimum of five votes in the case of abstentions. The majority vote to carry a decision should include a minimum of two of the four members from the USA, USSR, China and India. The chairman's vote would count no more and no less than the vote of any other member.

Impact on the Security Council As the proposed Peace Council would be responsible for many of the present functions of the Security Council, the latter body would assume a much lower profile. In effect, its principal remaining function would be periodically to elect the members of the Peace Council. This would appear to be a relatively painless and inexpensive way of disposing of a body which has failed the intent of the founders of the United Nations.

7 A Treaty for the Compulsory Arbitration of International Disputes

The need for a treaty A major objection to the abolition of war is that, taken in isolation, it would tend to favour the status quo and, as there are still many injustices and deep grievances in the world, this would result in great frustration. For instance, the abolition of war between nations would preclude external military assistance to an armed rebellion against a non-democratic regime, or against one that upheld a grossly unjust economic system in which there were great extremes of wealth and poverty. This frustration might well undermine the peace programme if no safety-valve mechanism was provided. The safety-valve proposed here is the agreement of all nations, in advance, that they would accept the decisions of the World Court as arbiter in international disputes. This acceptance would have to be mandatory and there could be no reservations or exceptions.

Since the middle of the nineteenth century an increasing number of nations have been willing to accept third-party arbitration or rulings of the World Court in cases of their own choosing. However, there has always been resistance by some governments to compulsory arbitration because of an overriding concern to preserve national sovereignty.[31] There are two powerful arguments against such a position in the context of this programme. Firstly, as indicated above, restraint of national sovereignty is the price that has to be paid for peace, and peace has to be the first priority on principle. Secondly, the World Court is a professional body which has a good track record of independence and evenhandedness. Indeed, an Independent Commission on Respect for International Law reported to a US Senate committee in 1986 that:

Most informed observers regard the behaviour of the World Court as very professional, especially when compared to any other major organ of the United Nations System.[32]

In exchange for agreeing to compulsory arbitration of disputes, governments would gain tremendously, through enhanced protection against direct assault and interference in their internal affairs by aggressive nations. Great nations as well as small nations would gain – for example, through the elimination of international terrorism. There is therefore every likelihood that the system would be equitable, and each nation should have the satisfaction of knowing that all others are subject to the same conditions.

The right of appeal   To deal with the most vital cases pertaining to the territorial integrity of a nation, such as a ruling to hand over land to a neighbouring country or to a minority seeking independence, it would be appropriate to have a system of appeal to the World Peace Council.

Human rights issues   Some of the most common grievances that will need to be relieved by the safety-valve system relate to human rights. This term is used here in the broad sense of the United Nations Universal Declaration of Human Rights, which covers not only the civil and political rights that are normally the main concern of capitalist democracies, but also the social and economic rights that are more often the interest of Socialist countries. By their very nature, economic rights take longer to implement than civil and political rights, especially in poor countries; in such cases nations would therefore have to be given an extended timetable, no doubt with benchmarks along the way, for the implementation of appropriate measures. It would also be important that grievances could be raised by individuals and private groups as well as by national governments. Finally, in the interests of objectivity and justice a violation of human rights would have to be treated as a legal matter and therefore be referred to the World Court, rather than to one of the political bodies of the United Nations.

An increased workload for the World Court These proposals regarding compulsory arbitration would require a considerable strengthening of the World Court, since there would inevitably be an increase in the number and complexity of the cases it handles. It would also acquire the additional function suggested above of trying national officials charged with ordering the use of weapons of mass destruction or the invasion of another country, as well as individuals charged with acts of international terrorism. There are, of course, precedents for such international trials of persons accused of crimes against humanity, of which the most notable were those held at Nuremberg after World War II.

Enforcement of World Court decisions To enforce the rulings of the Court, the World Peace Council should have the authority to call on member nations to apply sanctions against any nation which refuses to accept its decisions. There is also no doubt that to defuse potentially explosive grievances, sanctions would need to be applied in human rights cases, at least those involving gross violations.[33] Such sanctions would obviously have to be graduated according to the importance of the matter in hand.

Support for conflict resolution institutions The work of the Court would need to be supplemented as much as possible by institutions which assist in conflict resolution. It is, of course, preferable that disputes between nations should be settled by mutual agreement, if necessary with the assistance of a third party, rather than through the compulsory judgement of the Court. Techniques for mediation and conflict resolution are now used increasingly at all levels of society, for instance in family and industrial courts. In the 1970s they were used in a number of well publicised cases, including a dangerous hostage situation in Washington, D.C; and they have been used in international relations since the beginning of the nineteenth century, for instance to resolve differences between the United States and Great Britain concerning the Canadian border. An interesting development in recent years has been the addition of problem-solving approaches to the array of conflict resolution techniques. These new approaches can be used when other techniques are not appropriate – for instance to facilitate major social and political change or to handle issues, such as national pride and self-identity, which are non-negotiable. One of the most well known examples of the application of problem-solving techniques to international relations occurred in the 1970s, when the London-based Centre for Analysis of Conflict worked with Malaysia, Indonesia and Singapore to resolve an important dispute.

8 A Treaty to Establish an International Peace Force

A standing United Nations peace force   The effectiveness of military sanctions against an aggressor nation would be greatly enhanced if the United Nations were to have its own armed peace force, in addition to the designated national forces mentioned below. Such a force would be particularly useful for medium-intensity operations such as blocking the advance of an invading army or counter-attacking against an invader. No doubt the nations of the world would insist that the force should be kept small, at least until a democratic world government was established to keep it under close supervision. For the immediate future, during the early stages following the international abolition of war, a small elite force would be sufficient. A total of 50,000–100,000 personnel, with the capability of moving to any part of the world at short notice, might be sufficient to start with. The establishment of such a small permanent United Nations force would be a precedent for a true world police force at a later stage, a force strong enough in itself to guarantee the security of all nations.

The character of the peace force Military personnel in the permanent UN force should preferably be recruited as individuals, rather than as national units, so that all units down to platoon level are of international composition. Initially, this United Nations force could be armed with light defensive equipment, like all national forces. However, as confidence grows, consideration might be given to the provision of heavy offensive equipment, such as tanks and first-line military aircraft, in order to improve its capacity to make powerful counter-attacks if an invader should refuse to withdraw. All nations would be required to give the force priority right of passage when moving to counter an aggressor, as well as any forms of assistance necessary while in their territory.

Designated national forces So long as the United Nations peace force remains small, supplementary national units will be required to help it perform effectively. These would be intended for service with the United Nations during international emergencies or at other times when a large international force might be needed, for instance as a barrier between nations lacking trust in one another. The United Nations would need to have the strength to apply military sanctions against even the largest of nations. This suggests that a military force of at least one million personnel would have to be available at any one time. The designated national units would be made available on a rotating basis, for periods of perhaps two years, with contributions graduated in size according to national capacity. They would need to be clearly identified and given advance briefing and training, so that they could function efficiently in an international emergency. It would be important to avoid a situation in which the enforcement of United Nations sanctions resulted in only one or two nations being pitted against the aggressor, because this could undermine the perception that action was being taken by the world community as a whole. At any one time forces should be provided by a minimum of ten to twenty countries, with no single country providing more than a fixed maximum proportion, for example one-quarter or one-third. Such arrangements would, of course, be a considerable improvement over the present ad hoc arrangement, whereby the UN attempts to meet each emergency as it arises.

9 A Treaty to Establish an Independent Peace Fund

Why a fund is needed The above proposals would clearly involve an expansion of the United Nations' peacekeeping budget, in order to support a new World Peace Council, a permanent United Nations peace force, an inspectorate to supervise disarmament and the application of sanctions, and a heavier workload for the World Court. In addition, emergency economic assistance would probably be needed by countries subjected to aggression. It is important that the United Nations should not be hampered in carrying out these specialized and vital peacekeeping functions as a result of delays or refusals by member nations to pay their annual assessments, as sometimes happens now. For these purposes the United Nations should be given an independent and automatic source of income. This would, of course, be subject to normal budgeting and auditing procedures, like every other type of international expenditure.

Sources of income One possible source of income would be a tax on all minerals, such as oil and coal, taken from the earth or from the sea. In support of such a tax it is not unreasonable to argue that these non-renewable resources are, in a sense, the property of all mankind and do not belong exclusively to those who happen to live in the right place or to those who process them. An alternative possibility would be a small percentage sales tax to be applied uniformly in all countries. This would have the advantage of simplicity and approximate economic justice, because the rich countries would obviously pay far more per head than the poor countries. The collection of these taxes would have to be supervised by teams of third-party auditors reporting to the United Nations. The sums involved would almost certainly be much less than the savings realized in the medium and long term by the implementation of disarmament proposals – and as previously noted, the world now spends about 5 per cent of its total annual product on military affairs.

Additional uses for the fund The fund should be large enough to provide not only for the administrative expenses of the United Nations' additional peace-keeping functions, but also for a reserve from which temporary assistance could be given to countries suffering unduly as a result of abiding by a sanctions directive. It would also be desirable to make the fund large enough to provide a stable source of additional economic assistance to the world's poorest countries. This would contribute to the gradual elimination of one of the main underlying causes of conflict between nations.

10 An Equal Role for Women in the Peace Process

To strengthen the implementation of the seven proposed treaties, three general support actions might be considered. The first of these concerns the role of women.

As discussed earlier, there are at least two important reasons why women have a valuable role to play in the peace process. First, for physiological, social and historical reasons, women as a group have a special perspective and insight which strongly inclines them to peaceful conduct of public as well as individual relations. Consequently, it is vital that women who take part in the peace process do not become 'substitute men' – a major risk while public affairs are dominated by men – but remain firmly committed to feminine values. This will become easier as women approach numerical parity with men both in the peace process and in public affairs in general.

This leads to the second reason why it is desirable for women to be involved in the peace process. Equality of representation for women, half the world's population, in confronting the most important single item on the public agenda would reverse an age-old injustice against one of the world's largest oppressed groups. This example would make oppression in general more difficult and therefore enhance the prospects for lasting peace.

Just as peace must be the highest priority for diplomacy, similarly – because of the special role of women in the process – it should also be the highest priority of the women's movement. This would win the movement wider support and provide it with a basis for worldwide unity. With such support, women would be able to win many of their goals in areas of life where they are still treated unequally – just as wartime service won women in Western nations the right to vote in the first half of the twentieth century.

There are two other aspects of women's role in the peace movement which should be mentioned. First, they need to familiarize themselves with the technical details of peace proposals and military matters so that they are not at a disadvantage when persuading men of the rightness of their point of view. Secondly, active feminists will have a major responsibility in mobilizing mass support for the peace movement among the women of the world, since they know best what will attract the interest of other women, of whatever background; in particular, there is a need to reach the least well-off levels of society in all nations, capitalist, Socialist and Third World. In addition to logical arguments for placing peace at the top of the public agenda, there is a need to express issues in personal terms, both with regard to goals and means to attain those goals. All this suggests infinite opportunities for women to work for peace: not only in diplomacy, the peace movement, the media, law, education, social and economic development and the women's movement itself, but even in the home, the shopping place and parent-teacher meetings, etc.

11 Education of World Citizens

The second supportive action concerns education. It is essential to strengthen the consciousness of people everywhere that they are world citizens as well as citizens of their own particular country. One effective way to achieve this would be to institute compulsory classes at all levels of the education system (primary, secondary, tertiary and adult) in all countries. Such classes would deal with the eradication of prejudice, appreciation of the diversity of cultures, world history and other themes demonstrating the oneness of mankind. They would teach people to distinguish legitimate patriotism that creates a sense of worth and self-respect from nationalism which causes division and destruction; identify the causes of conflict in society; and explore how such conflicts can be resolved peacefully.[34] It is critically important that all sections of the political spectrum be invited to help contribute to this exercise so as to avoid the present perception in certain countries that campaigning for peace is somehow vaguely 'treasonable'. Such an international curriculum could be supported and made more effective by encouraging all types of cultural exchanges between countries.

12 The Elimination of Practices which Aggravate International Tension

The third supportive action is the elimination of activities which arouse suspicion and hostility between nations.

This positive programme of education in world citizenship needs to be complemented by a conscious and voluntary effort by all nations to eliminate wanton hostile propaganda against others. This does not imply censorship or silence about injustices perpetrated by others. What it does mean is applying a positive approach and encouraging other countries to eliminate grievances, rather than expressing self-righteous delight in the fact that they follow unjust practices. One particular area of activity which arouses immense suspicion and intensifies hostility between nations is the work of the 'dirty tricks' departments of secret service agencies. All nations, especially the super-powers, should be urged to conclude bilateral or multi-lateral agreements banning such activities. No doubt the gathering of information on other nations by secret services will continue to be considered an important aspect of security, at least until the establishment of a democratic world government. However, quite apart from the moral dimension, 'dirty tricks' such as the propagation of 'disinformation' and the deliberate destabilization of other governments should be rejected as extremely prejudicial to world peace.

PART THREE

Practical Considerations

CHAPTER 4

A Timetable for Peace

The question now remains as to whether it is possible to implement such a programme by the end of the century. In this writer's view the answer is surely yes. A timetable for implementation of the programme might have four distinct stages.

First, capitalizing on the good work that has been done around the world during the United Nations International Year of Peace (for instance, the widely publicized project of runners who carried a 'peace flame' around the globe), within three or four years it should be possible to build up a true world peace movement united on general principles, with branches in every nation and supported both by expert bodies and by ordinary people in all the countries of the world.

The second stage would be for the governments of all nations to convene a world assembly with a single item on its agenda: namely, to put an end to war between nations by the end of the millennium. Such arrangements should not require more than one year.

The third stage would be for the world assembly to consult on and draw up the seven treaties designed to: (i) outlaw war; (ii) abolish offensive weapons; (iii) define sanctions which would automatically be taken against any nation waging war; (iv) create a World Peace Council; (v) make arbitration of international disputes mandatory; (vi) establish a standing United Nations peace force; and (vii) organize an independent peace fund for the United Nations. Simultaneously, the peace process could be enhanced by (a) giving women an equal role; (b) initiating a worldwide education programme to promote a sense of the oneness of humankind; and (c) putting an end to the deliberate aggravation of international tension. Bearing in mind the priority mandate of the world assembly, this third stage should not take more than three or four years.

The fourth stage would be for the treaties to be ratified by the assemblies and governments of the members of the United Nations. With constant pressure from the world peace movement, made up of the ordinary people of the world, it is not unreasonable to expect that the majority of nations would complete this process within another three or four years.

This timetable suggests that the seven proposed treaties could be the law of the world by the year 2000. Even before this has happened, nations could start planning and implementing new military policies based on the hedgehog defence approach so that the destruction of offensive weapons can proceed with all speed once the treaties are law and no nation will be left feeling insecure or unprotected. In fact, if all went well, nations might wish to start the process of destruction of offensive weapons before all the treaties are ratified. This work would have to proceed simultaneously in all countries, in accordance with a predetermined schedule, so that approximately the same ratios are maintained until all such weapons have been destroyed; it should take place as quickly as possible, perhaps over a period of two years. These precautions would minimize the possibility of a temporary 'window of advantage' for any side at any stage in the process. It is possible that there may be technical difficulties in disposing quickly of the thousands of weapons of mass destruction which are now in existence, but there should be no problem in eliminating their threat to peace by destroying all the vehicles which could deliver them, such as missiles, aircraft and submarines.

CHAPTER 5

The Global Challenge and the Individual

As noted in the preface, the main purpose in presenting these suggestions is to assist the peace debate in moving from vague generalities and diverse concerns to the planning and implementation of practical solutions, founded on the basis of fundamental principles concerning the oneness of mankind and the nature of man.

The second purpose is to encourage the reader to become actively involved in the peace issue by emphasizing that:

i) just as in the nineteenth century it was possible, by a combination of consciousness raising and legislation to bring about the voluntary abolition of the institution of slavery though several thousand years old, so too it is possible to abolish the scourge of war by the end of this millennium if there is a will to do so;

ii) there is an opportunity for each one of us, powerful and humble, rich and poor, man and woman, young and old, to play an effective and vital role in this process;

iii) the opportunity implies responsibility. If the writer or the reader does nothing, then who will?

What actions can the individual take? The range of possibilities is very wide and, of course, opportunities vary with individual situations and capacities. But there are some obvious actions that we all might consider:

1) Work on ourselves each day so that increasingly we radiate love and peace through our attitudes, speech and actions. This does not have to be dramatic for those who live in undemonstrative cultures, such as parts of Europe and North America, and a low key approach would no doubt be the most effective.

2) Improve our knowledge of all the issues involved in the peace process so as to increase our effectiveness as representatives of peace. Let us not be content with vague sentiments. To assist in this endeavour, the bibliography lists some basic sources of information and ideas on peace issues.

3) Become involved in the peace movement. If there is no local organization, consider joining together with friends and acquaintances to form one.

4) Use our influence to encourage the peace movement to take a global view and to be fair and even-handed in its presentations and policies. Persuade it to adopt tactics of consultation and conciliation, rather than confrontation.

5) Encourage local authorities to include peace and the oneness of mankind in the syllabus of all education establishments. Offer to assist with such classes ourselves, if we feel competent to do so.

6) Encourage women's organizations to put peace at the top of their agenda and in effect become part of the worldwide peace movement.

CHAPTER 6

Summary of Underlying Themes

Past discussion of peace issues has often been hampered by fragmentary argument, obsession with detail rather than principle, and a lack of both vision and realism. To cut through this dense undergrowth of words, certain basic themes have been adhered to in drawing up the suggestions in this book. In making a critical analysis of the suggestions, the reader may wish to bear these themes in mind.

1 A focus on key global principles that can unite nations, rather than on local 'peace' issues which cause division and alienate an important sector of the political spectrum.

2 An integrated system to avoid the weaknesses associated with piecemeal approaches taken in isolation. For example, if the elimination of offensive weapons is to be a credible policy, it must be linked with the introduction of hedgehog defence systems and a strong code of sanctions to be applied automatically by the entire international community. In addition, to prevent the abolition of war leading to the accumulation of grievances against the status quo, there must be a safety-valve system for the compulsory arbitration of disputes by the World Court, with no exceptions or reservations.

3 Simple but significant concepts to reduce argument and division:

    a) the absolute abolition of war between nations, allowing for no prevarications or exceptions for 'just wars';

    b) the abolition of all offensive weapons, which are relatively easy to identify, in all countries without exception.

4 A realistic approach to the enforcement of peace, providing for:

    a) effective monitoring of disarmament;

    b) strong self-defence measures for each nation;

    c) realistic and effective collective security.

5 The settlement of disputes in an objective environment:

    a) political disputes to be adjudicated by a new World Peace Council, not by the Security Council or the General Assembly of the United Nations;

    b human rights grievances to be heard by the World Court, not by the politicized United Nations Human Rights Commission.

6 A focus on the solution of immediate critical prob-

lems. This means postponing important but medium-term issues which might otherwise obscure immediate problems and lead to a delay in their solution. Important issues which would be postponed until war is abolished include:

a) extensive reform of the United Nations;

b) subsequent steps towards genuine democratic world government based on sound moral principles;

c) the establishment of a fully-fledged world police force;

d) a comprehensive programme to eliminate the principal causes of political, social and economic injustice;

e) the adoption of a world auxiliary language.

7 Involvement of ordinary people from every nation and background to give support and encouragement to leaders and experts.

8 An emphasis on an equal role for women both as a matter of justice and because of their unique qualities which naturally incline them to peace.

9 Cultivation of the concept of world citizenship through the introduction of classes in schools, colleges and universities throughout the world that will teach the ideals of the peace movement and the unity of mankind.

Appendices

The Quest for Peace: A Short History of the Peace Movement

The dream of peace between nations is as old as civilization. It is a dream that for millennia has been associated with the ethical teachings of the great religions of the world. However, a dream was one thing, reality another. For most of recorded history war has been a routine of life, and peace has rarely been established over a wide area or for an extended period of time except under the powerful empires such as those of China and Rome. Even then peace was relative rather than absolute, and it was founded on force and fear rather than on a sense of community.

During the early Middle Ages, a new institution arose in Europe which gave some hope of a greater peace than that previously experienced under the old empires: the universal church under the leadership of the Pope in Rome. ('Universal' of course meant Western Europe, since Europeans were barely conscious of the rest of the world.) For several hundred years, rulers of European states would, for the most part, recognize the spiritual supremacy of the Pope and would on occasion defer to him in settlement of disputes between themselves. This fragile unity in Western Europe lasted for a few hundred years before being destroyed by the Reformation in the sixteenth century. With the collapse of the universal authority of the church, the rulers of states became sovereign in every respect, de jure as well as de facto. The era of the modern sovereign state and international anarchy is generally dated from the Treaty of Westphalia in 1648, which brought to an end the religious wars of the Reformation.

The legal anarchy that ensued soon began to cause concern among enlightened intellectuals, and over the next two hundred years a number of works were published which explored ways of remedying the situation. These writings ranged over many of the themes which have since become a routine part of the peace debate: arbitration and regular international conferences to discuss mutual problems (Hugo Grotius, 1583–1645); an international legislature and international laws (William Penn, 1644–1718, and Jeremy Bentham, 1748–1831); the importance of human rights and the need for a formal international convention denouncing war (Immanuel Kant, 1724–1804); sanctions against aggressors (Abbé de St Pierre, 1658–1743, and Jean-Jacques Rousseau, 1712–78); inspection and verification of the size and composition of the armed forces of states (Kant); and the creation of an international army to enforce the peace (William Bellars, 1654–1725). However, these scattered voices were crying in the wilderness and it is virtually impossible to detect any impact on the practice of international relations before the beginning of the nineteenth century. It was not until the end of the Napoleonic wars that statesmen, let alone ordinary citizens, began

98

to talk about the principle of peace as if it might become a realistic possibility.

The Birth of the Modern Peace Movement

Revulsion against the carnage of the Napoleonic wars prompted the founding of a series of 'friends of peace' societies in Great Britain and North America, of which the first was the New York Peace Society, established in 1815. The two earliest non-government international peace conferences were held in London in 1843, with participants drawn from Great Britain and North America, and in Brussels in 1848 with representatives from a wider range of countries. The first international peace organizations were La Ligue Internationale et Permanente de la Paix, founded in Paris in 1867, and La Ligue Internationale de la Paix et de la Liberté founded in Geneva in the same year. The latter was the more radical, for it emphasized that peace could only be lasting if based on just principles such as national self-determination, democracy, observation of basic human rights and the introduction of mass public education. The international peace movement was given what might be called a backbone with the establishment of the Bureau Internationale de la Paix in Berne in 1891. Under a series of able administrators the Bureau was to become a useful clearing house for discussion of ideas and problems relating to the peace issue.

The nineteenth-century peace movements were supported by a multitude of voluntary international bodies advocating international cooperation. One of the first was the Red Cross movement, founded in 1864 by a Swiss citizen, Jean-Henri Dumont. He had witnessed the Battle of Solferino, between the armies of France and Austria, and had been shocked by the casual lack of concern for the wounded. Other international organizations that were significant for the evolution of the struggle for peace during the nineteenth century included the International Institute of Law (1874), the International Arbitration League (1885) and the International Parliamentary Union (1889). In addition, there were two other initiatives of interest. One was the creation of an international language, Esperanto, by Ludovic Zamenhof (1859–1917), who from his experiences as a Polish Jew living in the Russian Empire became convinced that a common language for all peoples would be a powerful force for removing the political, social and economic barriers that divide the nations of the world. The second was the establishment of an annual international peace prize by the Swedish scientist and manufacturer of explosives, Alfred Nobel (1833–96). Popular interest in the peace issue was also promoted by two highly publicized books: *Lay Down Your Arms* (1889) by the Austrian baroness Bertha von Suttners[35] and *The Great Illusion* (1910) by the Englishman, Norman Angell.

The Congress System and the Hague Convention

The emergence of an international peace movement during the course of the nineteenth century was paralleled by some modest but nevertheless significant initiatives in diplomacy. The first such development was the so-called 'Congress' system created by the Allied powers in 1815 after their defeat of the Emperor Napoleon. The Allies were not only concerned with settling the issues pertaining to the Napoleonic wars, but wanted to establish an informal arrangement whereby in future they would meet together periodically to discuss any difficulties that might arise, with a view to reducing tensions and the risk of war. The distinguished English historian C. K. Webster described the second Congress, held at Aix-la-Chapelle in 1818, as 'the first ever held by the Great Powers of Europe to regulate international differences in times of peace'.[36]

The formal Congress system only lasted a few years, essentially because the Eastern European empires, Russia, Prussia and Austria, tried to use it to resist the spread of national independence and democracy, against the wishes of a large proportion of the population of Europe as well as the governments of Great Britain and France. Nevertheless, its spirit did not die out entirely and throughout the nineteenth century there was a series of international congresses to discuss various issues such as the Balkan disputes and the division of Africa amongst the imperial powers. In the words of Alfred Zimmern, the noted authority on international law, the Congress system was 'the repository of a tradition under which peace between the Great Powers was a habit and a general war unthinkable.'[37]

It was in accordance with this tradition that Tsar Nicolas II of Russia invited his fellow heads of state to meet at The Hague in 1899 to discuss disarmament,[38] the rules of war, and the arbitration of disputes between nations.[39] There was a consciousness of the dawn of a new century, and a desire to mark this event with some dramatic gesture in the direction of peace and progress. Barbara Tuchman in *The Proud Tower*[40] notes: 'People felt awe at the turn of the century, as if the hand of God were turning a page in human fate.' Unfortunately, perhaps inevitably, the conference did not live up to the hopes raised and there was little or no progress on the first two items on the agenda.[41] However, there was a positive development with regard to the third item when the powers agreed to a 'Convention on the Pacific Settlement of International Disputes'. The Convention embraced three themes: (i) the use of the good offices of a third-party nation for mediation of disputes between two other nations; (ii) the use of commissions of inquiry in cases of international disagreements; and (iii) the establishment of a permanent Court of Arbitration. The latter institution was gravely hampered in practice because it had no compulsory authority and could only intervene in a dispute when invited to do so by the participants. Nevertheless, it did represent a significant, if small step forward in the direction of the critical concept of a World Court. Two other aspects of the Hague Conference are worth noting. First, the great powers invited smaller powers to send representatives (a total of twenty-six sovereign states had representation), a change of attitude from the days earlier in the century when the great powers tended to treat the smaller ones as of no consequence. Private observers, including some representing the peace movements, were also permitted to attend. The other aspect of note was the agreement to hold another conference sometime in the future. Accordingly, a second conference was held at The Hague in 1907 which had on its agenda rules of war on land and at sea, disarmament matters, some aspects of the procedures for investigating international disputes and, most interesting, a major effort on the part of the US government to strengthen the Court of Arbitration and to make its use compulsory. Unfortunately, no agreement was reached on any of these issues and the next meeting, scheduled for 1915, was never held – because by then Europe was in the middle of the Great War.

The Beginning of International Cooperation

Though diplomacy failed in its direct efforts to maintain peace, there were several other diplomatic developments in the nineteenth century that represented an indirect approach to the issue and set important precedents for the future. The first was the beginning of international cooperation with regard to various social, economic and technical matters, which in the long run served to strengthen the sense of interdependence between nations, thus highlighting the absurdity of war. Two of the earliest instances of this type of cooperation were the establishment of the International Telegraph Union, founded in 1865, and the much more successful Universal Postal Union, founded in 1874. Other international institutions established before 1914 included a permanent office in Brussels to monitor information on slavery (1890); the International Institute of Agriculture (1905), created to gather information on trends in the market for agricultural produce; and the International Office of Public Health (1909), set up to coordinate quarantine measures and the international standardization of drugs. One other secondary development that served to reduce tensions between nations was the beginning of a movement for cooperation at the regional level. The first organization in this field was the Pan-American Union, founded in 1889 after long decades of struggle on the part of New World statesmen, particularly from the southern part of the continent. Years later there were to follow such important regional and inter-continental organizations as the British Commonwealth of Nations (1907), the League of Arab States (1945), the European Community (1957),[42] the Organization for Economic Cooperation and Development (1961), the Organization of African

103

Unity (1963), the Association of South-East Asian Nations (1967) and the Caribbean Community (1973).

The League of Nations

The disaster of the Great War – in which some 20 million people died, more than in any previous conflict – prompted renewed efforts by the governments of the world to conduct international relations in a more rational and constructive way. The major initiative came in 1918 from the American President, Thomas Woodrow Wilson, whose Fourteen Points fore-shadowed a new world order. In essence these proposed a peace settlement based on four general principles: (i) national self-determination; (ii) an association of the nations of the world which would provide mutual guarantees of territorial integrity and independence; (iii) a regime of open covenants (i.e. no secret treaties between nations); and (iv) a reduction in armaments. The central powers agreed to an armistice on this basis, but in the hurly-burly of power politics and high passions induced by the great pain and suffering of the war the original concepts were, to a considerable degree, modified and twisted.

Nevertheless, a new international order was created, centred on two new institutions: the League of Nations and the Permanent Court of Justice which was in effect an improved version of the Court of Arbitration. The Covenant of the League, which was incorporated into the Treaty of Versailles (1919), comprised eight basic principles:

1) Every member recognized and promised to respect the integrity and independence of every other member.

2) War was recognized as a threat to all and was automatically a subject for deliberation by the League.

3) All members bound themselves to submit all disputes to peaceful arbitration, and in no case to go to war for at least three months, thus providing a reasonable time to settle the issue peacefully.

4) All nations bound themselves to take common action against any state making war in violation of the Covenant, and to come to the assistance of any member subjected to aggression. Initially, sanctions would be economic, but if they should fail to restrain the aggressor, then military action could be taken, together with expulsion from the League.

5) Members should reduce their armaments to the minimum necessary for security, bearing in mind the collective security mentioned above.

6) All members would conduct diplomacy in the open, and would not make secret agreements. Any existing secret agreements would be automatically abrogated.

7) Former colonies of the defeated powers would be the responsibility of the League, but would be administered on its behalf by nominated countries until such colonies were ready for independence.

8) Members agreed to cooperate for the common good in a wide range of economic and social fields, such as international transportation, postage and other communications, commerce, international health matters, conditions of labour, and the suppression of the international traffic in slavery.

In the last half-century the League of Nations has been severely criticized because it failed to prevent World War II. That criticism has obscured the fact that the League was, despite its flaws, a giant step forward for civilization on the road towards world order and peace. The Covenant of the League set forth more clearly than ever before agreed fundamental principles of international relations on such matters as the peaceful settlement of disputes, collective security, reduction of armaments, open diplomacy, and cooperation in economic and social fields. It provided a regular forum, backed by an international civil service, for discussion of mutual concerns. Perhaps above all, it helped to raise consciousness amongst a growing number of people that ultimately they were world citizens, not just members of their own nations. Furthermore, the League had several important successes, especially in its early years, which demonstrated that an international organization could indeed function effectively when the majority of its members wished it to do so. Thus the League was successful in defusing several disputes between European nations in the 1920s, and the Court of Justice gave twenty-three judgements in cases brought to it between 1921 and 1945. The League played a role in the negotiation of the Locarno Pact of 1925, which gave an international guarantee of the Franco-German frontier – a development that helped considerably to reduce international tensions for several years. The League was also instrumental in securing the approval of many nations for the Kellogg–Briand Pact of 1928, which 'renounced war as an instrument of national policy'. Of course, the Kellogg–Briand Pact was severely deficient in so far as it did not provide for enforcement, and indeed its terms have been repeatedly broken by signatory powers. Nevertheless, in the broader perspective it should be seen as an important precedent in the whole process of persuading peoples and their governments that war is an unacceptable way of conducting international relations. Another field of endeavour where the League was able to make a useful contribution to peace in the longer perspective was with regard to disarmament. Most notable was the 1921 Washington Naval Treaty, signed by the governments of the five leading naval powers of the time, which led to genuine and substantial reductions in naval armaments for a period of nearly two decades. Though the League was not directly involved in negotiations for that treaty, it was clearly inspired by the spirit and principles of the League's Covenant. In addition, the League's Preparatory Commission on Disarmament, working in the 1920s, was able to reach agreement on several broad principles for disarmament negotiations: agreement on the need for budget ceilings for military expenditures, a limitation on the number of years of service for conscripts, a limitation on manpower in land, sea and air forces, a renunciation of chemical and bacterial warfare, and the establishment of a permanent disarmament commission to monitor adherence to any agreement.[43]

Many explanations have been given for the failure of the League. In the writer's view the main cause was twofold. First, the Versailles peace settlement left three of the seven great powers of the time deeply dissatisfied, a feeling which was compounded by the Great Depression. The discontented powers reverted to militarism and believed that they could achieve their goals by force and in defiance of the principles of the League. On the other hand, and this is the second point, there was no united front to resist aggression. It is conceivable that the three discontented powers might have

107

been constrained if the four remaining great powers had been able to work together in the League along with the fifty or so smaller powers which were members. However, one of the four (the USA) never joined the League and another (the USSR) was excluded from the League until 1935. It is hardly surprising therefore that the two remaining powers, Great Britain and France, dithered in their support of League principles; in the short run at least the odds must have seemed risky, and the temptation to revert to traditional diplomatic manoeuvring must have been very powerful. Unfortunately, it has to be added that the peace movement of the time did not help the situation, since it failed to see the link between the maintenance of League principles and militarily strong democracies.[44]

By comparison with these broad issues, technical deficiencies in the Covenant such as the formal link with the Treaty of Versailles, the voting system, the failure to create an international police force, and the absence of a statement on human rights and the equality of race were all, it would seem, comparatively minor. After 1930 and the onset of the Great Depression there seemed to be an inevitability about events, and the effectiveness of the League steadily declined under the buffeting of a series of international crises: Manchuria (1931), Ethiopia (1935–6), the Rhineland (1936), Austria (1937), Czechoslovakia (1938), Poland and Finland (1939).

The United Nations

World War II, like the Napoleonic wars and the Great War, provoked a strong revulsion against military solutions and an equally strong desire among ordinary people for international relations to be conducted peacefully. This feeling was reinforced by a growing appreciation of what was implied by the nuclear bomb. One thing was clear: international institutions would have to be strengthened to make them more effective instruments for maintaining peace. Rather than try to reform the discredited League, the victorious Allies opted to start afresh with a new organization, the United Nations. The UN was similar to the League in its structure: a two-tier assembly and council system, a professional international secretariat, and a permanent Court of Justice. To eliminate perceived weaknesses in the League's structure, more formal power was given to the five great powers, which alone could exercise a veto in the Security Council, and the Secretary-General was given a somewhat wider range of discretion to take initiatives in times of crisis. Much more significant was a conscious effort to tackle some of the underlying causes of war by putting greater emphasis on inter-national assistance to alleviate poverty and promote economic development, and by setting basic worldwide standards for human rights. The first of these themes resulted in the establishment of several new institutions such as the World Bank, the International Monetary Fund and the UN Development Programme, as well as the strengthening of several other institutions such as the Food and Agriculture Organization and the World Health Organization, all of which were to be coordi-nated by a new Economic and Social Council. The latter theme produced the Universal Declaration of Human Rights and a series of supporting conventions, as well as a special Human Rights Committee to monitor adher-ence to the standards agreed. Also of great importance was the fact that this time the international organiz-ations were to become almost universal in their

109

membership; most particularly, after a period of transition, they were to include all the great powers, including those which had been defeated during the war.

Looking back over the forty years or so since the foundation of the United Nations, there can be little doubt that it has made some very useful contributions to the work of upholding international law and reducing international tensions. On two occasions at least the UN assumed a high profile: in countering the invasion of South Korea in 1950 and in taking action to end anarchy in the Congo in 1960. In addition, there have been a large number of other occasions where the UN has been able, in a less dramatic fashion, to mediate a settlement of international disputes or to bring about temporary truces by sending in neutral peacekeeping forces. Such services have been particularly useful in facilitating the process of decolonization. Moreover, the World Court has given forty-two judgements in cases submitted to it between 1946 and 1984. Perhaps equally significant has been the unprecedented and voluntary transfer of a considerable amount of real resources between nations to alleviate poverty and promote development, both through the UN's multilateral agencies and through bilateral arrangements. One of the outstanding achievements of these programmes has been the 'green revolution', which has helped many countries to become essentially self-supporting in food production. Another has been the virtual eradication of a whole range of diseases such as cholera, yellow fever, yaws and trachoma. The work of the United Nations in the human rights field has had a significant impact on raising consciousness of this cause worldwide and thereby made abuse of ordinary people a more difficult exercise for oppressive governments.

Despite these achievements there is a widespread feeling that the UN has not been a success. The main disappointment, of course, is that, contrary to the high hopes of 1945, the UN has not been able to impose peace: wars seem to occur with the same frequency as before, and we all live in fear of nuclear disaster. The work of helping the poorest countries develop their economies and improve the standard of living of their peoples has run into a large number of difficulties. Thus the relatively modest goal set by the UN in its first 'Development Decade', that the rich countries should contribute 1 per cent of their annual gross national product as international economic aid, has never been reached in aggregate; indeed with each succeeding year such a goal recedes further and further from reality.[45] Partly this failure reflects a feeling in the rich countries that aid is not working very well and that much of it disappears into the pockets of corrupt politicians.[46] Similarly, there is disenchantment with the UN's work in the human rights field, as it never seems to take action even in the most blatant cases of abuse. There is also much criticism of the UN institutions themselves: they are seen to be flabby and ill coordinated, and the secretariat is accused of nepotism.

Clearly the UN is far from being a perfect institution and no doubt it merits some criticism. However, the main responsibility for the perceived failures of the UN rests with the member nations. It was they who decided in the first place, despite lessons from the League of Nations, not to give the UN adequate means to carry out its functions properly. Thus the UN was not given an armed police force or an independent source of income, and the World Court was not given compulsory powers of arbitration. Nevertheless, the UN could have been far more effective had its member nations

111

played the game according to the rules and given international order a higher priority. Indeed the great powers have made the Security Council virtually useless by abusing their right of veto, which they do not hesitate to use for even minor issues. Some of the great powers have also set an unfortunate example in ignoring the World Court, even though it is clearly in their interest that law and order in international relations be strengthened. The General Assembly has lost a lot of the respect it might have had as a real parliament of the peoples of the world through the insistence of the majority of Third World countries that it be used for empty bombast and unenforceable resolutions. Industrial countries, on the other hand, have for the most part failed to take seriously the responsibility they have for reducing starvation and extreme poverty in the Third World. Perhaps most irresponsible because so unnecessary and so obviously not in the interest of anyone, a number of countries have wantonly undermined the institutions of the UN by such practices as failing to pay their dues, insisting on nepotism in the staffing of the secretariat (instead of supporting recruitment based on merit), and encouraging hostility to the UN among their own peoples. Several sensible suggestions for reforming the UN to make it more effective and efficient have been blocked either by the superpowers or by blocs of other countries which clearly have in mind narrow self-interest rather than the good of the international institutions as a whole. In short, national governments, including some that are democratic, frequently fail to live up to their international responsibilities and indeed to their own finest traditions. There is clearly a need here, if the prospects for peace are to improve, for ordinary citizens and peace movements in general to play a much more active and informed role in holding governments to account for their actions vis-à-vis the United Nations.

Religion and Peace

As mentioned earlier, the idea of peace has often been linked to the teachings of the great religions and indeed one could not discuss the movements towards abolishing war without mentioning some of the salient contributions of world religions to this issue. While no one can dispute the fact that innumerable wars have been fought in the name of religion, nevertheless peace has always been given a special position in the original teachings of every great religion.

To the search for peace, all the religions of the world have contributed a belief in the spiritual and transcendental nature of man as a creature of God, a station which should distance him from showing acts of violence to his fellow human beings. Each has also brought essential ethical and social teachings designed to help mankind live in harmony. Added to this is the significant vision of the Golden Age of humanity that is painted in the holy scriptures of almost every religion. An example of this can be seen in the Bible, in the prophecies of Isaiah:

They shall beat their swords into ploughshares,
and their spears into pruning hooks;
nation shall not lift up sword against nation,
neither shall they learn war any more.

Within the Christian tradition, Quakers stand out as a major force for social change with their overriding belief in non-violence. They were preaching the gospel of pacifism as early as the seventeenth century, and

113

suffered persecution for their beliefs. As individuals they steadfastly refused to bear arms or to take any part in the waging of wars, believing warfare to be contrary to the will of God. The Quaker ethic has always encouraged its adherents to concern themselves with other people's sufferings. Concern has meant more than sympathy; it has meant practical help for people in need. The abolition of slavery, for example, was one of the major achievements of the nineteenth century in which the Quakers played a crucial part. All through the previous century, in England and America, Quakers were prime movers in the uphill struggle, first to put an end to the profitable trade in fresh slaves from Africa, and later to put an end to the profitable exploitation of slaves wherever they happened to be. The Quakers' moral conviction of the evil of slavery, their patience and struggle in the face of discouraging circumstances decade after decade, and their objectivity in carefully gathering facts and statistics on slavery were the main factors which can account for their historic success.

While the Quakers and many other individuals in the West were engaged in their attempt to abolish slavery, in the nineteenth century the main religious organizations of the world were in disarray and did not give much moral leadership on peace. Nevertheless, many of those involved in the peace movement were inspired by the broad principles of religion and some of the more progressive Christian sects, such as the Methodists and the Quakers, were strongly represented in the movement. Another development which, although relatively obscure at the time, had a long-term significance for the peace movement was the founding in 1863 of the Bahá'í Faith.

The special significance of this new religion in the

context of the peace movement is that it is very explicit in stating that one of its main goals is the achievement of world peace based on justice; indeed, its principles and teachings amounted to a plan of action to achieve that end far more comprehensive and more practical than that provided by any other philosophy or religion. Furthermore, the appeal of this new religion was broad, as is shown by the fact that today its 5 million adherents are drawn from virtually every race, nation, class and religion.

Like all the major religions, the Bahá'í Faith has as a fundamental principle the belief that humanity is one family, and its teachings are specifically designed to remove the barriers that obstruct a realization of that concept. Thus Bahá'ís are required to revere equally the founders of all the world religions. Together these religions are seen as one progressive movement giving unfolding guidance to humanity as civilization evolves, so providing a point of unity for adherents of all religions. The Bahá'í Faith also maintains that when religious practice contradicts science, it is the practice which is wrong, because religion and science are two sides of the same truth; thus the scientist can indeed embrace religion in good conscience. It further advocates that each person's search for the truth must be based on intellectual and emotional integrity; and that there must be a conscious effort to abolish prejudice against those who are different from ourselves, and to appreciate the enrichment of civilization which comes from the diversity of culture; that civilization will only have a proper balance when there is equality between men and women, socially, economically and politically; and that a peaceful society requires just and loving individuals.

Accordingly, in common with other religions, the

Bahá'í Faith puts emphasis on the cultivation of noble qualities (truthfulness, honesty, charity, etc.) as well as on the family, where the individual, as a child, learns a loving attitude towards others. This theme is epitomized in the teaching that the highest form of worship is service. A peaceful society also requires a just and united form of government. The Bahá'í community therefore organizes its affairs around democratically elected assemblies – thus avoiding that major source of conflict, the individual leader. Assemblies function at the local, national and world levels according to principles of universal consultation rather than confrontational debate. To further maintain unity, Bahá'ís are enjoined to be loyal to all established governments and not to partake in partisan politics. The ultimate goal is the establishment of a federal world commonwealth in which most public decisions will be taken at the local community level in accordance with the general policy guidelines set by a democratically elected world government with responsibility for promoting unity, equal opportunities, fair distribution of resources and, above all, peace. In summary, the overall approach is world peace based on a spiritual renaissance and the essential foundations of unity and justice. In 1867–8 letters advocating these principles were sent to the leaders of the major nations of the world by the founder of the Bahá'í Faith, Bahá'u'lláh (1817–92).

Religion has continued to be a powerful force in the peace process in recent decades, although this has perhaps been obscured at times by public consciousness of the declining influence of some of the older religious institutions, especially in the West, on the one hand, and the rise of religious fanaticism on the other. One example of a religious initiative to reduce barriers between people, and thus indirectly to promote the cause of peace, has been the ecumenical movement, especially within Christianity. Another has been the issuance of statements on the direct question of peace by several religious bodies. Among the best known of such pronouncements have been Pope John XXIII's *Pacem in Terris* (1963) and the statement on disarmament issued by the American National Conference of Catholic Bishops (1982). In connection with the UN International Year of Peace, the Bahá'í community issued a statement called *The Promise of World Peace*, which was presented to the UN Secretary-General and to the heads of state or government of nearly every member nation of the UN; and it might be added that the international Bahá'í community and five national Bahá'í communities have received special commendations from the UN for their work in promoting the UN Year of Peace.

Peace Initiatives since 1945

What then of peace movements since World War II? The movements which for long attracted the most attention were those primarily concerned with the nuclear issue, such as the Campaign for Nuclear Disarmament in the UK. These movements clearly served a useful purpose in heightening public consciousness of the dangers at hand and in challenging the comforting bromide-style language of orthodox bodies who suggested that nuclear weapons could be used and that there could be winners in a nuclear war. However, these peace movements tended to repeat mistakes made by peace movements in the inter-war period, in that their focus was narrow and not evenhanded; and they lacked credibility with the majority in Western countries because the policies they advocated, such as unilateral

117

disarmament, were regarded as benefiting the Soviet bloc at the expense of the West.

However, in recent years there have been instances of mass concern that have been more universal in their approach. One of the most spectacular occurred on 17 June 1982, when there was a demonstration outside the UN headquarters in New York which appealed to the governments of the world to take serious actions to reduce armaments. With an attendance of 750,000, this demonstration for peace was perhaps the largest single gathering of people in history; and in the humanitarian field, the worldwide support given in 1985 to the campaign initiated by the pop singer Bob Geldof to raise funds to help the starving in Ethiopia is a heart-warming example of a growing sense among young people of the oneness of mankind.

These positive developments have been underpinned by the work of a multitude of organizations,[47] many of which are highly informed on particular issues connected to peace. Some of these have status as non-government organizations (NGOs) at the United Nations, which gives them a degree of access to diplomats involved in peace issues. Two of the most distinguished such bodies are Amnesty International (founded in 1961) and International Physicians for Prevention of Nuclear War (founded in 1980), both of which have been awarded the Nobel Peace Prize.

In addition, there have been a series of well argued books and television presentations which have heightened public consciousness of the reality of war and the absolute necessity for peace in this age of mass destruction weapons. Those involved have included Aurelio Peccei and Ervin Laszlo, both members of the Club of Rome; Jonathan Schell, author of *The Abolition* and *The Fate of the Earth* (the latter is one of the best

118

accounts of the nuclear winter theory); Gwynne Dyer, author of the book and TV programme *War*; Lynn H. Miller, author of *Global Order: Values and Power in International Politics*; Greville Clark and Louis Solm, authors of *World Peace through World Law*; Benjamin Ferencz, author of *A Commonsense Guide to World Peace*; and Gerald and Patricia Mische, authors of *Toward a Human World Order*.

It is generally accepted that one of the first steps that would help to ease tensions in the world and therefore make it easier to start tackling the underlying causes of conflict, would be to reduce the burden of armaments. This is a subject which has been debated almost continuously since the founding of the United Nations, with particular emphasis on the arms of the two superpowers and, to a lesser extent, the other great powers. Immense mistrust has made progress extremely difficult, indeed one of the most important stumbling blocks at the technical level has been the question of verification. After two decades of immobility, things began to change as tensions between the superpowers eased. There was a series of international agreements of which perhaps the most important were the treaties to ban nuclear tests in the atmosphere (1963) and to prevent the proliferation of nuclear weapons to third parties (1968). In the seventies, the two superpowers agreed on limitations to strategic weapons (Strategic Arms Limitation Treaties I and II) and on anti-ballistic missile systems. Though important as precedents, these treaties were decidedly weak in several respects. The test treaties still allowed underground testing, so that development of nuclear weapons continues; and the non-proliferation treaty has failed to prevent perhaps as many as half a dozen non-nuclear powers from acquiring the ability to make such weapons, a development which considerably increases the risk for all humanity. Furthermore, the two SALT treaties, as their titles imply, only put a limit on the pace of the armaments race; they did not put it into reverse. It is encouraging that in the current round of negotiations between the superpowers the latter deficiency is being corrected. The Intermediate Nuclear Forces Treaty (INF) and the proposed Strategic Arms Reduction Treaty (START) both provide for significant reductions in the number of nuclear weapons and delivery systems possessed by both sides. This is a promising beginning, but it has to be recognized that even if they are implemented the world will still be at great risk and much more will have to be done to achieve a stable peace.

Statistics on War and Peace

1 Nuclear Weapons of the Superpowers

I Growth of US and Soviet Strategic Nuclear Missile and Bomber Forces, 1945–85

	1945	1950	1955	1960	1965	1970	1975	1980	1985
Warheads									
USA									
Missiles				68	1,050	1,800	6,100	7,300	7,900
Bombs and ALCMs	2	450	4,750	6,000	4,500	2,200	2,400	2,800	3,300
Total	2	450	4,750	6,068	5,550	4,000	8,500	10,100	11,200
USSR									
Missiles				some	225	1,600	2,500	5,500	9,300
Bombs and ALCMs			20	300	375	200	300	500	600
Total			20	300	600	1,800	2,800	6,000	9,900
Delivery systems									
USA									
Bombers		some	400	600	600	550	400	340	263
ICBMs				20	850	1,054	1,054	1,050	1,020
SLBMs				48	400	656	656	656	648
ALCMs									1,080
USSR									
Bombers			some	150	250	145	135	156	160
ICBMs				some	200	1,300	1,527	1,398	1,398
SLBMs				15	25	300	784	1,028	924
ALCMs									200

		USA	USSR
(A) **Strategic** (see above)		11,200	9,900
(B) **Intermediate Range**		236	1,435
(C) **Tactical**			
Artillery shells		2,400	900
Anti-submarine warheads		2,000	600
Anti-ship cruise missile warheads		0	1,000
Battlefield ballistic missile warheads		300	1,600
Anti-aircraft missile warheads		200	300
Anti-ballistic missile warheads		0	32
Anti-demoliton mines		600	some
Non-strategic bombs		4,000	4,000
		9,500	8,432
	Total	20,936	19,707

In addition there are believed to be considerable reserve stocks giving all told a total of about 50,000 for the two superpowers together.

Source: Robert McNamara, *Blundering into Disaster*, Pantheon Books, 1987.

2 A Comparison of the Conventional Forces of the Warsaw and NATO Alliances

	NATO[1]	Warsaw[2] Pact	Warsaw Pact in Relation to NATO: NATO = 100.0
A Personnel			
Ground Forces	2,400,000	2,300,000	95.8
Air Forces	640,000	730,000	114.1
Total	3,040,000	3,030,000	99.7
B Equipment			
Tanks	22,200	52,200	235.1
Artillery	11,100	37,000	333.3
Combat Aircraft	3,292	7,524	228.6

[1]*NATO Countries*
1 Belgium
2 Denmark
3 France
4 Germany (West)
5 Greece
6 Iceland
7 Italy
8 Luxemburg
9 Netherlands
10 Norway
11 Portugal
12 Spain
13 Turkey
14 UK
15 USA

[2]*Warsaw Pact Countries*
1 Bulgaria
2 Czechoslovakia
3 Germany (East)
4 Hungary
5 Poland
6 Romania
7 USSR

Source: *The Economist*, 28 November 1987 (based on data from the International Institute for Strategic Studies).

3 Real Increases in World Defence Expenditures, 1976–1985
(Expressed in billions of constant 1980 US dollars)

Region	1976	1980	1985	Percentage Increase 1976–1985 (10 yrs)
NATO	233.3	256.3	327.7	40.0
Warsaw Pact	135.7	144.3	160.1	18.0
Other European Countries	14.1	15.4	16.6	17.7
Middle East	39.1	41.2	49.6	26.9
South Asia	5.7	7.1	9.1	59.6
Far East	21.3	27.4	34.8	63.4
Oceania	3.8	4.3	5.4	42.1
Africa	12.9	14.8	12.7	–1.6
Central America	1.9	2.9	3.8	100.0
South America	9.9	11.3	13.3	34.3
Total	477.7	525.0	633.1	32.5

Source: *Stockholm International Peace Research Institute Yearbook on World Armaments and Disarmament*, Oxford University Press, 1986.

4 Defence Expenditures as a percentage of GDP/GNP
(1984 data)

Defence as % of GDP/GNP	No. of Nations and States					
	Africa	Americas	Asia	Europe	Oceania	Total
Less than 1%	2	5	–	1	–	8
1–1.99%	4	8	6	6	3	27
2–2.99%	16	6	1	5	1	29
3–3.99%	2	1	2	9	–	14
4–4.99%	3	2	1	3	–	9
5–5.99%	4	–	4	2	–	10
6–6.99%	–	1	2	–	–	3
7–7.99%	1	2	2	2	–	7
8–8.99%	2	1	2	–	–	5
9–9.99%	2	1	–	–	–	3
10% and over	3	1	13	1	–	18
Total in survey	39	28	33	29	4	133
Not surveyed	12	7	6	4	8	37
Grand Total	51	35	39	33	12	170

Countries spending more than 10% of GDP/GNP on defence are:

Africa: Angola (16.9); Ethiopia (11.4) and Somalia (11.3).

Americas: Nicaragua (11.7).

Asia: Iran (12.3); Iraq (51.1); Israel (24.4); Jordan (13.4); Korea, North (10.2); Lebanon (19.2); Mongolia (11.5); Oman (24.2). Qatar (13.1); Saudi Arabia (20.9); Syria (15.1); N. Yemen (17.8); S. Yemen (16.3).

Europe: USSR (13–15).

Source: *The Military Balance 1986/87*, International Institute for Strategic Studies, 1986, and *The Economist*, 6 June 1987, with regard to USSR.

123

5 Military Manpower in 1984

| Size of Manpower | No. of Nations and States | | | | | |
	Africa	Americas	Asia	Europe	Oceania	Total
None	–	2	–	–	–	2
Less than 10,000	19	6	3	2	2	32
10,000–99,999	17	14	16	10	2	59
100,000–199,999	3	4	4	6	–	17
200,000–299,999	1	1	3	3	–	8
300,000–399,999	–	–	1	3	–	4
400,000–499,999	1	–	2	2	–	5
500,000–599,999	–	–	–	1	–	1
600,000–699,999	–	–	1	1	–	2
700,000–799,999	–	–	1	–	–	1
800,000–899,999	–	–	2	–	–	2
900,000–999,999	–	–	–	–	–	–
1,000,000 and more	–	1	3	1	–	5[1]
Total in survey	41	28	36	29	4	138
Not surveyed	10	7	3	4	8	32
Grand Total	51	35	39	33	12	170
Total manpower of surveyed countries (millions)	1.8	3.6	11.7	10.1	0.1	27.3[2]

[1]*Nations with largest armed forces are*: USSR (5.1 million); China (3 million); USA (2.1 million); India (1.3 million); and Vietnam (1.2 million).

[2]In addition there are some 42.6 million reservists and 30.3 million in paramilitary forces.

Source: The Military Balance 1986/87, International Institute for Strategic Studies, 1986.

6 Rich and Poor Nations of the World

Gross National Product per capita, 1983

| Wealth Category[1] (US dollars) | No. of Nations and States | | | | | | Percentage of Total | |
	Africa	Americas	Asia	Europe	Oceania	Total	Countries	Population
5500 and above	1	3	13	19	3	35[2]	20.6	15.6
1635–5499	5	11	9	13	0	37[3]	21.8	20.7
401–1634	17	20	8	1	9	56[4]	32.9	13.5
400 and less	28	1	9	0	0	42[5]	24.7	50.2
Total	51	35	39	33	12	170[6]	100.0	100.0

[1] World Bank categories as used in *World Bank Atlas*, 1985.

[2] Essentially Western Europe, North America, Japan, Australia and New Zealand, together with rich oil producing nations in other parts of the world. Twenty-four of the thirty-five have per capita wealth of US$10,000 or more.

[3] Includes USSR (population of 272 million) and Brazil (population of 130 million).

[4] Includes Indonesia (156 million population) and Nigeria (94 million population).

[5] Includes Bangladesh (95 million), China (1022 million), India (733 million) and Pakistan (90 million).

[6] All the independent states of the world except for the Vatican. The figure does not include about 40 overseas territories and islands, most of which are very small. The most important are: Hong Kong, Macao and Namibia. Of the 170 independent states, 157 are members of the United Nations.

Source: World Bank Atlas, 1985 and *The World in Figures* (*Economist*), 1976.

7 Official Development Assistance for Selected Countries 1960–1985

A OECD Countries	ODA as a percentage of GNP				Percentage of ODA Given as Multilateral Assistance (1980)[1]
	1960	1970	1980	1985	
1 Netherlands	0.31	0.61	1.03		25.5
2 Norway	0.11	0.32	0.85		42.6
3 Sweden	0.05	0.38	0.79		26.8
4 Denmark	0.09	0.38	0.73		45.9
5 France	1.35	0.66	0.64		17.3
6 Belgium	0.88	0.46	0.50		24.0
7 Australia	0.37	0.59	0.48		27.4
8 Canada	0.19	0.41	0.43		38.3
9 West Germany	0.31	0.32	0.43		35.3
10 Great Britain	0.56	0.41	0.35		44.8
11 Japan	0.24	0.23	0.32		40.6
12 USA	0.53	0.32	0.27		38.8
13 Italy	0.22	0.16	0.17		89.2
OECD Total	0.51	0.34	0.38	0.35	35.2
B OPEC Countries					
Kuwait		5.81	3.88		16.2
Saudi Arabia		5.02	2.60		26.1
OPEC Total		4.04	1.47	0.60	19.2
C Official UN goal	1.00	0.70	0.70	0.70	

[1]The remainder would be bilateral assistance
Source: OECD

8 Basic Indicators of Health in the Nations of the World

(A) Life Expectancy at Birth (1982 data)

Continent:	No. of Nations and States and Life Expectancy in Years						Countries not surveyed	Grand Total
	70 and above	60–69	50–59	40–49	39 and below	Total		
Africa	1	7	18	20	5	51	0	51
Americas	12	19	4	0	0	35	0	35
Asia	7	15	7	6	1	36	3	39
Europe	28	1	0	0	0	29	4	33
Oceania	2	3	4	0	0	9	3	12
Total	50	45	33	26	6	160	10	170
% of countries	31.3	28.1	20.6	16.3	3.7	100.0		
% of population	20.2	41.8	31.4	5.9	0.7	100.0		
GNP per capita (US dollars)							Per cent of total	
399 or less	0	6	9	20	5	40	25.0	
400–1634	5	25	19	6	1	56	35.0	
1635–5499	21	13	2	0	0	36	22.5	
5500 and above	24	1	3	0	0	28	17.5	
Total	50	45	33	26	6	160	100.0	

Source: World Bank Atlas, 1985

(B) Changes in Life Expectancy and Infant Mortality, 1950–1985

(I) Average Life Expectancy at Birth

Period	World	Dev Nations	LDCs	Africa	Americas Latin	Americas North	Asia East	Asia South	Europe	Oceania	U
1950–55	46.0	65.0	41.0	97.8	51.0	69.1	42.7	33.9	65.3	60.8	6
1980–85	59.5	73.1	57.3	49.4	64.2	74.4	68.4	54.9	73.1	67.9	7
% change	+29.3	+12.5	+39.8	+30.7	+25.9	+7.7	+60.2	+37.6	+11.9	+11.7	+1

(II) Infant Mortality in First Year of Life (rate per 1000 live births)

Period	World	Dev Nations	LDCs	Africa	Americas Latin	Americas North	Asia East	Asia South	Europe	Oceania	U
1950–55	156	54	180	191	125	29	182	180	62	67	7
1980–85	78	16	88	112	62	11	36	103	15	31	2
% change	–50.0	–70.4	–50.1	–41.4	–50.4	–62.1	–80.2	–42.8	–75.8	–53.3	–6

Source: Population Trends, No. 47, Spring 1987, HMSO, London.

9 Adult Literacy Rate in Nations of the World

(Status in 1960s and 1970s)[1]

Percentage of Adults Literate	No. of Nations and States						Percentage of Total	
	Africa	Americas	Asia	Europe	Oceania	Total	Countries	Population
90–100%	0	8	1	22	3	34[2]	25.2	25.5
80–89%	0	8	4	2	0	14[3]	10.4	26.8
70–79%	0	4	2	2	0	8	5.9	4.0
60–69%	2	4	5	1	0	12[4]	8.9	9.2
50–59%	7	2	3	0	0	12	8.9	2.7
40–49%	4	1	2	0	0	7	5.2	1.9
30–39%	8	0	2	0	1	11[5]	8.1	18.6
20–29%	6	1	7	0	0	14[6]	10.4	6.3
10–19%	13	0	2	0	0	15	11.1	4.2
0–9%	7	0	1	0	0	8[7]	5.9	0.8
Total in survey	47	28	29	27	4	135	100.0	100.0
Not surveyed	4	7	10	6	8	35		
Grand Total	51	35	39	33	12	170[8]		

[1]Literacy means ability to both read and write. Adult means aged 15 or over.
[2]Includes USA, USSR and Japan.
[3]Includes China.
[4]Includes Brazil and Indonesia.
[5]Includes India.
[6]Includes Bangladesh and Pakistan.
[7]Saudi Arabia has the lowest rating (3 per cent) in the survey.
[8]Excludes the Vatican and various overseas territories and islands

Source: World Handbook of Political and Social Indicators, by Charles Lewis Taylor and David A. Jodice, Yale University Press, 1983.

Peace Questionnaire

DRAFT OF A QUESTIONNAIRE WHICH MIGHT BE
SENT TO HEADS OF GOVERNMENT OF ALL
MEMBER COUNTRIES OF THE UNITED NATIONS

A If all other governments of member countries of
the United Nations were prepared to agree to the
actions listed below, would your government be
prepared to do so as well?

		YES	NO
1	Agree to the convening of a special World Peace Assembly with the sole purpose of ending war between nations by the end of the century?	. . .	. . .
2	Sign and ratify an international treaty outlawing war between nations?	. . .	. . .
3	Sign and ratify an international treaty abolishing all offensive weapons, on the understanding that defensive weapons would still be permitted?	. . .	. . .
4	Sign and ratify an international treaty to apply sanctions without reservation		

against any nation which wages war in
defiance of the treaty outlawing war? . . . . .

5 In view of the unsuitability of existing
United Nations institutions, sign and
ratify an international treaty to establish
a new World Peace Council,[1] to direct
the application of such sanctions? . . . . .

6 Sign and ratify an international treaty
agreeing to compulsory arbitration of all
international disputes by the World
Court, with the right of appeal to the
World Peace Council in decisions
requiring the transfer of territory? . . . . .

7 Sign and ratify an international treaty
to estabish an international police force
consisting of designated national units
and a small permanent United Nations
unit? . . . . .

8 Sign and ratify an international treaty to
establish an international peace fund for
the United Nations, to pay for the
United Nations peace force and
expenses arising from the application of
sanctions against nations waging war? . . . . .

[1] The proposed World Peace Council would have nine members,
each elected for six-year terms on a staggered basis, with three
members changing every two years. There would be one member
each from the USA, USSR, China and India. Another four would
come from the four most highly populated continents: Africa, the
Americas, Asia and Europe. These eight would be elected by the
Security Council. The ninth member would be chairman and would
be elected by the other eight. Decisions would be by a two-thirds
majority, which would have to include affirmative votes by at least
two of the four members from large nations.

9 Undertake to involve women equally with men in national contributions to the work of abolishing war between nations?   . . .   . . .

10 Undertake to include a standard international education course teaching the oneness of mankind in the curriculum of all educational institutions in your county?   . . .   . . .

11 Undertake to abstain from provoking international tension through hostile propaganda and comment on other nations?   . . .   . . .

B If there are any reservations or qualifications concerning your answers to the above questions, please describe them briefly in the space below:

Notes

1   Ervin Laszlo, Ed., *Goals for Mankind*, Hutchinson, 1977.

2   The Universal House of Justice, *The Promise of World Peace*, Oneworld Publications, 1986.

3   The war between Iran and Iraq has already lasted seven years, longer than either world war, and has cost at least one million lives.

Civil wars involving considerable outside participation include those in Afghanistan, Angola, Cambodia, Chad, El Salvador, Guatemala, Lebanon, Morocco, Mozambique, Nicaragua and Sri Lanka. In addition, there are 'private' civil wars such as those in Ethiopia, Peru, Sudan and Uganda.

Another category of violence is that of terrorism. Often the motivation is nationalism, as in the case of such groups as the Armenians, the Basques, the Corsicans, the Croats, the Gurkhas, the Irish, the Kurds, the Palestinians, the Sikhs and the South African blacks. In other cases, terrorism is a product of left-wing ideology, e.g. in Belgium, Colombia, France, West Germany, Italy and

Venezuela.

Yet another manifestation of daily international violence is the assault on civilized society of criminal gangs, particularly those involved with drugs. These have become so powerful in the Americas and Asia that they are able to terrorize legal institutions with impunity, and to act like medieval barons or kingmakers between the established governments and revolutionary groups.

Not far below the surface of peace, there are a dozen or more situations where extreme tensions threaten to break out into violence at any time, for instance those that exist between India and China, India and Pakistan, China and Vietnam, Israel and her neighbours, North Korea and South Korea, etc.

Over-arching the whole scene of contemporary war is the forty-year-old all-threatening hostility between the two superpowers and their allies.

4   Jonathan Schell, *The Abolition*, Avon Books, 1984.

5   Mikhail Gorbachev, as quoted in the *Washington Post*, 10 December 1987.

6   Military and economic power are not the only tools of international influence. Experience suggests that nations which pursue a policy based on ethical considerations (e.g. respect for international law and order, support for human rights and democracy, and support for soundly based international economics and cooperation) win influence and friends far in excess of what can be accounted for on the basis of military or economic power.

7   Henry Kissinger, as quoted in *Newsweek*, 21 December 1987.

8   Adolf Hitler, as quoted in *The Promise of World Peace*, p.93.

9   H. B. Danesh, *Unity: the Creative Foundation of Peace*, The Association of Bahá'í Studies, 1986.

10 *The Promise of World Peace*, p.82

11 Ibid., p.86.

12 Ibid., p.94

13 Men have shown considerable ingenuity in rationalizing such a state of affairs. One religious explanation is that woman is the temptress (Eve etc.), and must therefore be carefully controlled for the sake of public order and peace. As men have always been the aggressors in sexual matters, this is a clear case of self-serving hokum.

    A second argument is that women are intellectually as well as physically inferior. Just to make sure, they were denied education. Of course, as soon as women managed to get equal education, they showed that this argument was nonsense by more than holding their own with men.

    A third argument has been that woman's proper role is in the bedroom, the nursery and the kitchen, and that public affairs should be left to men. This argument also falls down when consideration is given to the awful mess men have made of public affairs, especially in the international arena.

14 Mary Midgley and Judith Hughes, *Women's Choices*, St Martin's Press, 1983.

15 There are scholars who argue that there were societies in prehistory, before the coming of the written word, in which women were in equal part-

nership with men and which were non-warlike and non-hierarchical in social structure. Societies of this sort in South East Europe (the Minoan civilization of ancient Crete being the most well known) were overrun by male-dominated nomadic hordes sweeping in from the vast lands of central Asia. A recent summary of this point of view can be found in *The Chalice and the Sword* by Riane Eisler, Harper & Row, 1987.

16 *Women's Choices*, p.27.

17 Margaret Thatcher, as quoted on p.31 of *Women's Choices*.

18 Joni Seager and Ann Olson, *Women in the World*, Pan Books, 1986.

19 *The Promise of World Peace*, p.98.

20 George Kennan, as quoted in *Blundering into Disaster* by Robert McNamara, Pantheon Books, 1987, p.85.

21 Bertrand Russell, *Has Man a Future?*, Penguin Books, 1961, pp.46–7.

22 An explanation of the Bahá'í view can be found in H. B. Danesh's *Unity: The Creative Foundation of Peace*.

23 Lynn H. Miller, *Global Order*, Westview Press, 1985, p.118.

24 Danesh, *Unity*, p.39.

25 See for example, O. P. Ghai, *Unity in Diversity*, Charles Skilton, 1986.

26 *Einstein on Peace*, Ed. O. Nathan & H. Norden, Avenel Books, 1981, p.617.

27 Lynn H. Miller, *Global Order*, p.109.

28 Benjamin B. Ferencz, *A Commonsense Guide to World Peace*, Oceana Publications, 1985, p.86.

29 Robert McNamara, *Blundering into Disaster*, p.80.

30 There is a big gap between the populations of the four largest countries (China 1,022 million; India 733 million; the USSR 272 million; and the USA 234 million) and the next largest countries (Indonesia 156 million; Brazil 130 million; and Japan 119 million). To provide for unforeseeable changes in the relative position of the great powers it might be necessary to include a clause in the constitution of the Council allowing for a periodic review of the representation, say every five or ten years. In such reviews, population should be the most important factor; but it might be appropriate to allow for other factors too, so that the truly most influential and important powers are properly represented on this supreme council of the world.

31 Only forty-six out of the 160 or so member nations of the UN have agreed to accept the compulsory jurisdiction of the World Court, and many of them have insisted on important caveats which gravely weaken their real commitment.

32 From the 1986 statement of the Independent Commission on Respect for International Law to the Committee on Foreign Relations of the United States Senate. (Quoted on p.36 of *Breakthrough*, Vol. 8, Nos 1–2, published by Global Education Associates, 1986.)

33 The voting record of member countries on the UN Human Rights Commission is notorious for

'political trading', with little regard for evidence of human rights abuse.

34 Some useful ideas on curricula for raising a generation of world citizens can be found in 'Educating for a Global Future', in *Breakthrough*, Vol. 8, No. 3–4, published by Global Education Associates, 1987.

35 Leo Tolstoy said this book was as important in the struggle for peace as *Uncle Tom's Cabin* was in the struggle to abolish slavery.

36 C. K. Webster, *The Foreign Policy of Castlereagh*, p. 121.

37 Alfred Zimmern, *The League of Nations and the Rule of Law*, 1939, p. 78.

38 This was the first instance of discussions of multilateral disarmament. However, there were precedents in bilateral disarmament agreements; one of the earliest and most enduring of these was the 1817 treaty between Great Britain and the USA to keep the Canadian–US border unfortified.

39 There had been no previous discussions of multilateral arbitration, but there were many instances of bilateral arbitration arrangements. Alfred Zimmern states that there were over 200 such arrangements between 1794 and 1914, mostly dealing with minor disputes involving the constitutional great powers: France, Great Britain and the USA.

40 Barbara Tuchman, *The Proud Tower*, Macmillan, 1966, p.267.

41 With regard to rules of war, it was agreed to ban: (i) the firing of projectiles from balloons; (ii) the

135

use of asphyxiating gases; and (iii) the use of expanding bullets.

42 The EC has led to so much economic, social and political integration among the nations of Western Europe that it is now virtually inconceivable that these nations could ever again go to war against each other – a remarkable development after thousands of years of armed strife.

43 The subsequent Disarmament Conference of 1932 was a complete failure, not least because France gave Hitler a perfect excuse for stage-managed anger when it proposed that disarmament start with a five-year freeze. This would have put Germany at an obvious disadvantage, and it must be presumed that the French government really did not want disarmament at that time. Another important aspect of the Conference was the failure to reach agreement on definitions of offensive as distinct from defensive weapons.

44 It is always difficult to draw parameters for the peace movement because it is so obviously closely related to issues of justice. It is therefore relevant when describing the peace movement in the thirties to make at least passing mention of the concept of civil disobedience as an alternative to violence, which was advocated by Mahatma Gandhi at that time. This technique has since been developed, most notably by Martin Luther King and the US civil rights movement in the fifties and sixties, and is now advocated by some as a way to discourage war. The theory is that an aggressor would think twice about invading another country if warned in advance that occupation would be

countered by non-cooperation on so massive a scale as to make government virtually impossible. There is, of course, much scepticism as to whether such techniques would work against aggressors as ruthless as the Nazis. However, it is an option that might well be useful in certain circumstances and should therefore not be dismissed out of hand.

45 See Appendix II.7.

46 For instance, a poll in the United States in 1979 showed that 91 per cent of those polled believed that 'too much of our foreign assistance is kept by the leaders of poor countries and does not get to the people.' (Quoted on p.15 of *The IDA In Retrospect*, Oxford University Press, 1982.

47 The Swarthmore College (USA) Peace Collection lists some 1,500 peace groups in some fifty nations (*World Enclyclopaedia of Peace*).

Bibliography

Clark, Grenville & Sohn, Louis *Introduction to World Peace Through World War*, World Without War, USA, 1984.

Danesh, H. B. *Unity: The Creative Foundation of Peace*, The Association of Bahá'í Studies, Canada, 1986.

Doherty, James E. & Robert L. Pfaltzgraff Jnr. *Contending Theories of International Relations: A Comprehensive Survey*, 2nd Edn., Harper & Row, USA, 1981.

Dyer, Gwynne *War*, Bodley Head, England, 1985.

Dyson, Freeman *Weapons and Hope*, Harper & Row, USA, 1985.

Ferencz, Benjamin B. *A Commonsense Guide to World Peace*, Oceana Publications, USA, 1985.

Huddleston, John *The Earth is but One Country*, Bahá'í Publishing Trust (UK), 1977.

Laszlo, Ervin, Ed. *Goals for Mankind*, Hutchinson, England, 1977.

Laszlo, Ervin and Yoo, Jong Youl *World Encyclopedia of Peace* (4 Vols), Pergamon Press, England, 1986.

Martin, Brian *Uprooting War*, Freedom Press, 1984.

McNamara, Robert *Blundering into Disaster*, Pantheon Books, 1987.

Miller, Lynn H. *Global Order: Values and Power in International Politics*, Westview Press, USA, 1985.

Mische, Gerald and Patricia *Toward a Human World Order*, Paulist Press, USA, 1977.

Peccei, Aurelio *One Hundred Pages for the Future*, Pergamon Press, England, 1982.

Reardon, Betty A. *A Comprehensive Peace Education: Education for Global Responsibility*, Columbia University Press, USA, 1988.

Reardon, Betty A. *Sexism and the War System*, Columbia University Press, USA, 1985.

Riggs, Robert E. & Jack C. Plano *The United Nations International Organisation and World Politics*, Dorfey Press, USA, 1988.

Rovine, Arthur W. *The First Fifty Years: The Secretary-General in World Politics 1920–1970*, A. W. Sychoff, Netherlands, 1970.

Schell, Jonathan *The Abolition*, Avon Books, USA, 1986.

Schell, Jonathan *The Fate of the Earth*, Avon Books, USA, 1982.

Sivard, Ruth Leger *World Military and Social Expenditure*, an annual publication by World Priorities, USA.

Tyson, J. *World Peace and World Government*, George Ronald, England, 1986.

The Universal House of Justice *The Promise of World Peace*, Oneworld Publications, England, 1986.

Walzer, Michael *Just and Unjust Wars*, Pelican Books, England, 1977.

Zimmern, Alfred *The League of Nations and the Rule of Law*, Macmillan, England, 1939.

TO UNDERSTAND AND BE UNDERSTOOD
A Practical Guide to Successful Relationships
Erik Blumenthal

To Understand and Be Understood presents a refreshingly original approach to social life today. Written by an internationally respected psychotherapist in a warm, anecdotal fashion, this book offers down-to-earth, workable advice for successful, loving relationships.

The author brings the reader a new understanding of himself and others based on simple, easy-to-use principles, illustrated throughout with real life examples drawn from years of professional practice. A valuable handbook for all those seeking more aware, understanding relationships in all spheres of their lives.

Erik Blumenthal, a practising psychotherapist, lectures at the Alfred Adler Institute in Zurich, and is currently President of the Swiss Society for Individual Psychology. He is the author of a number of books on child-rearing, self-education, marriage and old age.

ISBN 1–85168–004–7   paperback   160pp   £4.50   US$7.50

SCIENCE AND RELIGION
Towards the Restoration of an Ancient Harmony
Anjam Khursheed

Over the last two decades, exciting discoveries in modern physics have challenged scientists to reconsider some of their most basic assumptions about the nature of the universe – and of man. It is in the light of these recent developments that Anjam Khursheed, himself a research physicist at the European Centre for Nuclear Research (CERN) in Geneva, reviews the traditional conflict between science and religion in Western society.

Science and Religion is a fascinating and well researched account of that conflict, focusing on man's present predicament and escalating global problems. Of interest to both the scientist and the general reader.

ISBN 1–85168–005–5   144pp   paperback   £4.50   US$7.50

THE HIDDEN WORDS OF BAHÁ'U'LLÁH
Bahá'u'lláh

This exquisite collection of meditational verse is perhaps the best known work of the founder of the Bahá'í Faith, written in 1858 whilst exiled to Iraq from his native Iran. For years only a few hand-written manuscripts survived. Now, however, it has been translated into sixty-nine languages, with over 100,000 copies sold worldwide.

Designed by the award-winning Nicholas Thirkell, and selected as one of the best designed books in the world at the international exhibition of books in Germany in 1987, this is the first de luxe gift edition of a remarkable work which offers wisdom to guide every seeker through the constant struggle of the spiritual journey.

ISBN 1–85168–001–2   112pp   Cloth   £8.95   US$13.95

THE PROMISE OF WORLD PEACE
The Universal House of Justice

This beautifully produced, sumptuously illustrated book is an unusual mixture of fact, photographs and a plea for peace. In a world beset with escalating global problems it offers a verbal and visual presentation of the need for positive action.

The text, originally written and privately circulated by the governing body of the Bahá'í Faith, represents an analysis of humanity's current predicament and an outline of the attitudes and decisions which need to be adopted to secure world peace. Acclaimed by heads of state, politicians, royalty, religious leaders and philosophers worldwide, its noble and radical appeal to the better nature of humankind has been rendered into forty-five languages.

ISBN 1–85168–002–0   192pp   120 illns   paperback
£6.95   US$10.95

DRAWINGS, VERSE & BELIEF
Bernard Leach

Here we have a testament to a life spent discovering 'the unfamiliar groundwork of humanity in search of truth and beauty'. Born in Hong Kong in 1887, Bernard Leach was a potter of world renown whose life and work bridged the traditions of East and West.

Leach's sensitive illustrations and verse reflect a richly varied life travelling and living in both continents. The illustrations in this volume cover a period of sixty-three years, capturing in delicate pen and wash scenes of rugged English landscapes and lazy summer days, tranquil Japanese lakes, snow-capped peaks and busy harbours. The earliest poem dates back to 1907, penned by a young man of twenty, while the later verse reflects a man of mature years, sight failing, dwelling on the meaning of life.

This beautiful, cloth-bound gift edition combines the author-artist's delicate visual images and delightful verse with an impassioned profession of faith, to provide a rare insight into the personality of a great master craftsman.

ISBN 1–85168–012–8   160pp   82 illns   Cloth
£12.95   US$19.95

THE WAY TO INNER FREEDOM
A Practical Guide to Personal Development
Erik Blumenthal

The Way to Inner Freedom is a practical, down-to-earth guide to personal development. Written by an internationally respected psychotherapist in a warm, jargon-free style, this superb book offers a simple, step-by-step programme of self-discovery and self-education.

Life's everyday problems can cause stress, anxiety and frustration and often lead to difficulties in relating to others and even to oneself. In this positive and encouraging book Erik Blumenthal explains that freedom is an inner quality dependent on our own conscious choices.

The Way to Inner Freedom is for everyone seeking the freedom to control their own lives, to develop their inner potential, and to replace self-doubt with confidence, frustration with peace and a sense of purpose. Only you can change yourself; *The Way to Inner Freedom* shows you how.

ISBN 1–85168–011–X   144pp   paperback   £4.50   US$7.50

ONEWORLD PUBLICATIONS

Oneworld Publications publishes contemporary books on cultural, philosophical and social issues. We focus on peace and global concerns, personal development, the family, spiritual awareness, religious questions and the Bahá'í Faith. For further information about Oneworld Publications books, please write to the Mailing List Dept at Oneworld Publications, 1c Standbrook House, Old Bond Street, London W1X 3TD, England.

Some Oneworld titles you may enjoy:

Science and Religion Anjam Khursheed	US$7.50	£4.50	☐
To Understand and Be Understood Erik Blumenthal	US$7.50	£4.50	☐
The Way to Inner Freedom Erik Blumenthal	US$7.50	£4.50	☐
The Hidden Words Bahá'u'lláh	US$13.95	£8.95	☐
The Promise of World Peace The Universal House of Justice	US$10.95	£6.95	☐
Achieving Peace by the Year 2000 John Huddleston	US$5.95	£3.50	☐
Drawings, Verse & Belief Bernard Leach	US$19.95	£12.95	☐
The Secret of the Stolen Mandolin Barbara Larkin (Children's fiction)	US$3.75	£2.25	☐

All these books are available at your local bookshop or library, or can be ordered direct from the publisher. Just tick the titles you want and fill in the form below:

Name (Block letters) ⸻⸻⸻⸻⸻⸻

Address ⸻⸻⸻⸻⸻⸻⸻

⸻⸻⸻⸻⸻⸻⸻⸻

Send to Oneworld Publications, Cash Sales Department, 1c Standbrook House, Old Bond Street, London W1X 3TD, England.
Please enclose cheque or bank draft to the value of the cover price plus postage & packing:
UK: 15% for orders up to £20 and 10% for orders over £20. Maximum postage £5.
OVERSEAS: 15% on all orders.
All payments should be made in US Dollars or Pounds Sterling.